Kingston's BURIED TREASURES

A HISTORY REVISITED AT THE
LECTURE SERIES HELD AT
THE SENATE HOUSE, 2012–2016

Ed Ford, beloved Historian for the City of Kingston, has done more to preserve and protect the history of Kingston than anyone we can think of. He was an inspiration for the "Kingston's Buried Treasures" series and the featured presenter for two of its lectures. And he is, without question, the greatest ambassador for our local history that Kingston has ever known.

Edwin Ford

Born on April 15, 1918, Ed Ford has lived through six wars and countless armed conflicts. He has seen eighteen U.S. presidents come and go and he has lived through the Great Depression, the Great Recession and at least as many bumps in the road as the years he has behind him. Except for a few years here and there Ed has called Kingston his home since he moved here from his grandfather's farm in Highland in 1928. His devotion to our history and his personal example have been an integral part of our historical community for more than half a century. When the call of "progress" sought to erase the vestiges of our heritage, Ed was there, often by himself, to halt the machine. There were moments of great success and there were times of bitter disappointment. Yet through every up and every down, Ed maintained a generosity of spirit to which we can all aspire. For more often than not, it's the messenger and not the message that determines the success of the venture. And Ed has been an exceptional messenger.

This book is dedicated to Ed Ford, an admirable legacy, we hope, for a man who has done more than any other to preserve ours.

Thank you, Ed.

Kingston's Buried Treasures

Appreciation

"Kingston's Buried Treasures" would like to acknowledge
Kingston's New York State Assemblyman Kevin Cahill,
whose generous contribution helped
make this book possible.

Thank you, Kevin

Contents

Foreword

Thomas Cornell—industrial tycoon, congressman and founder of the Cornell Steamboat Company—was the inspiration for what became the lecture series "Kingston's Buried Treasures." A small, but fitting, legacy for a forgotten man who towered over Kingston's history for nearly a century.

"Kingston's Buried Treasures" was born on the belief that our history, particularly our forgotten history, mattered. It mattered in our community, it mattered in our state and our nation, and, in many instances, it mattered to the world. But matter it did, and with the hard work and dedication of a number of historic-minded individuals and the enthusiasm of a devoted audience, the "Kingston's Buried Treasures" lecture series was inaugurated on August 17, 2012 with a talk by Ted Dietz on Kingston's first settler, Thomas Chambers.

But "Kingston's Buried Treasures" also owes its start to a very special event held here in Kingston on April 20, 2012. On that date Kingston celebrated a most unlikely bicentennial—the 200th anniversary of the death of Founding Father, Ulster County resident, New York State's first governor and two-time United States Vice President George Clinton. The event brought together a wide variety of historical groups and individuals and resulted in a ceremony made as memorable for the beautiful early spring day as for the tributes of our dignitaries to Ulster County's favorite son.

With the momentum created by this event and relationships newly formed, we moved forward with the idea that a monthly series highlighting a different person, place or event in Kingston's history just might spark an interest in our oft-neglected past and a pride in the contributions of our forebears. This group originally consisted of myself, Ulster County Clerk Nina Postupack, Kingston City Historian Ed Ford, graphic designer Joe Tantillo, Ulster County Historian Anne Gordon, President of the Friends of Historic Kingston Pat Murphy and Kingston Common Council Majority Leader Tom Hoffay. Soon added were journalist Hugh Reynolds, Tom Kernan and Deana Preston from the New York State Senate House Museum, videographer Bob Rizzo and local historian Walt Witkowski, each of whose contributions proved invaluable to the success of the series.

You couldn't have found a more dedicated ensemble and for the next three and half years we were able to cover much of Kingston's history-from our first settler to our many prominent politicians and leaders, from freedom fighters to gilded era industrialists, from simple homes to palatial estates. With the help of friends, neighbors and an amazing group of presenters willing to share their efforts and knowledge we were able to travel through more than 360 years of Kingston's history and relive events from which we can be suitably proud. And we were most fortunate to have both a literary and video legacy of the series through the outstanding Kingston Times articles of Hugh Reynolds and the videos of Bob Rizzo. This book encapsulates "Kingston's Buried Treasures" through the eyes, the ears and the pen of Hugh Reynolds—a fitting and perhaps undeserved tribute to our efforts.

"Kingston's Buried Treasures" was without question one of the most rewarding experiences of my life and, I hope, has left our community a little better than when we began. Did we succeed? I'll leave the answer to you. But we sure had fun.

Enjoy.

Paul O'Neill

Kingston's
BURIED
TREASURES

George Clinton:
A Brief Sketch

Gov. George Clinton

The thumbnail sketch of the all but forgotten George Clinton typically reads: Patriot, Revolutionary War general, first governor of New York who served an unequaled seven terms, father of the state university system and its first chancellor, anti-federalist who opposed the Constitution but forced the subsequent Bill of Rights, Vice President under Jefferson and Madison.

As John P. Kaminski's 1993 biography *Yeoman Politician of the New Republic* dem-

> *"Clinton's legacy was a vibrant nation of states and people, just beginning to develop its unlimited potential of political and economic freedom."—*
>
> *John P. Kaminski*

onstrates, there was much more to this seemingly obscure figure. In that biography, Kaminski detailed Clinton's crucial role in what could be fairly considered one of the seminally significant "what-ifs" in American history.

The military situation in September 1777 found British General John Burgoyne running low on supplies and sorely pressed by ever-increasing American forces near Saratoga. Burgoyne pleaded for reinforcements from General William Howe, in command of occupied New York City. George Washington, headquartered near Philadelphia, recognized the threat and summoned Governor Clinton from military retirement to return as commander of the undermanned and poorly defended Highlands forts that Clinton had built south of West Point. Howe assembled a flotilla with 4,000 troops, but as an apparent feint, according to Kaminski, sent them toward Philadelphia. After patriots evacuated the capital, Howe turned his force back north and up the Hudson. To force a passage, Howe's army of regulars and Hessians would have to subdue forts Montgomery and Clinton. General Clinton, with only 600 defenders, held off the superior British force long enough to thwart Howe's plans.

The rest is history.

While many of Clinton's official papers were destroyed in the burning of Kingston and in the 1911 fire at the state museum in Albany, his public life is detailed in Kaminski's biography through contemporary accounts. Glimpses of the man emerge as well.

Born to a farm family in Orange County in 1739, Clinton for his entire career identified with "yeomen," farmers, merchants—what would become the middle class. His work as a surveyor and land speculator introduced him to future constituents far beyond his Ulster-Orange base.

Period portraiture depicts him as a robust man with a passing resemblance in stature to his friend and idol, George Washington. The two worked closely in the defense of the Hudson Valley during the war and were later partners in land speculation in the Mohawk Valley. They remained personal friends— Clinton named two of his five children after George and Martha Washington— despite sharp differences over the federal Constitution. While Kaminski does not speculate, it is possible Washington took advice from Clinton— by then New York's governor for more than a decade—in establishing the federal executive branch of government in 1789. At one point, Clinton was considered as Washington's vice president.

There is little mention by Kaminski of the courtship of Clinton and Cornelia Tappen, described as a "pretty little Dutch girl." She and her family attended the Old Dutch Reformed Church in Kingston; Clinton was raised as a Presbyterian but was not a regular church attendee. Like many of the Founders, he considered himself a deist.

Some controversy surrounds the Clinton marriage. Apparently due to difficulties with Old Dutch elders, the couple chose to elope. Crossing the frozen Hudson by horse-drawn sleigh in February 1770, they were married at a Reformed church in Germantown. Clinton held a reception for some friends shortly after.

Clinton as an early advocate of separation from England was a radical. While apparently not a member of the Sons of Liberty, he did according to Kaminski advocate the assassination of King George III.

As governor his treatment of loyalists, whom he saw as traitors to the cause, was considered harsh. Tory property was confiscated and redistributed to soldiers, their owners tarred and feathered and sometimes murdered. Many fled to Canada or England.

In war and peace and owing to governmental duties in New York, Albany and Washington, Clinton spent little time in Kingston. There is no record of his owning a home in Kingston. He lived with his in-laws, the Tappens, at the corner of Wall and North Front streets after his marriage, and he stayed at what came to be called "the governor's mansion" as a visiting governor. There is a state historic marker where the building once stood.

Kaminski depicts the Clintons as a devoted couple who rarely entertained at home because of Cornelia's fragile health. Cornelia died in March 1800. Clinton never remarried. His enemies portrayed him as rigid, uncompromising and controlling, his friends as a pragmatic man of principle. He served in dangerous times. For his first six years as governor, New York was under constant threat from British-occupied New York City and Tory, Indian and British threats on its frontiers. After the war, in a rough and tumble era of American politics, he faced constant attack from political enemies, including Federalists Alexander Hamilton, John Jay and Philip Schuyler (Hamilton's father-in-law).

Kaminski's concluding paragraph speaks to Clinton's place among the Founding Fathers: "George Clinton helped win America's independence. Subsequently he devoted his life to securing the triumph of republicanism, what we would call today democracy, uncontrolled by wealth or corruption. That America in 1812 was a democratic and diverse society and was on the verge of enormous economic expansion was in no small degree due to Clinton's

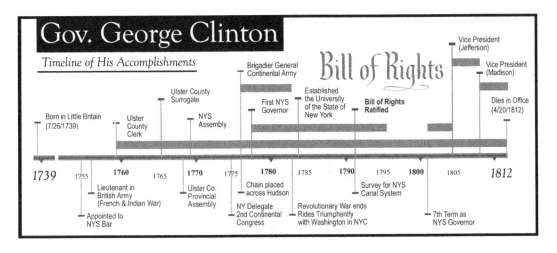

influence. His legacy was a vibrant nation of states and people, just beginning to develop its unlimited potential of political and economic freedom."

The 200th anniversary of George Clinton's death was celebrated in Kingston in April 2012 with reenactments, lectures, essays by schoolchildren, speeches by politicians and ceremonies at his grave in the Old Dutch Cemetery. The main lecture was delivered by Professor John P. Kaminski, director of the Center for the Study of the American Constitution of the University of Wisconsin–Madison. Dr. Kaminski is recognized as a leading scholar of that era. His 1993 biography of Clinton is considered by many the definitive account of Clinton's controversial life. (Excerpts are included in this piece.)

The city-wide Clinton celebration sparked a renewed interest in Kingston history. It was the impetus for the 41-month lecture series, "Kingston's Buried Treasures," upon which this book is based.

Brigadier General George Clinton during the Revolutionary War

1.

Thomas Chambers: The "Founder"

Early Esopus document

Foxhall Avenue and Manor Avenue are named for a red-headed early settler of Kingston. So were a street in old Rondout and an elementary school in the Town of Ulster. But few Kingstonians, other than a dedicated coterie of amateur historians and long-out-of-print books, recognize one of the community's first leaders, Thomas Chambers.

One of those local history buffs, New York City transplant Ted Dietz, gave a two-hour lecture on the life and times (1620–1694) of Chambers at the Senate House Museum on August 17, 2012. It was the first in a series of lectures on historic Kingston figures sponsored by the Senate House, the Friends of Historic Kingston and

> ### *"Somebody you'd want out front in a big fight."*

other historic-minded interests.

While seven men are historically associated with the founding of the Esopus colony in 1652, city historian Ed Ford considers Chambers *the* founder.

His was the first local deed recorded, at Fort Orange in 1653, for about 70 acres off North Manor Avenue where the Esopus veers north toward Saugerties. The original is on file at the Senate House.

"Chambers was a leader. That much has been well documented," Ford said. "They must have realized what they had here before they came down [from Rensselaerswyck]. He must have been the initiator. He was that kind of man. He was looked up to by others."

Literally. Dietz described Chambers from historical records as "a big red-headed guy, a fighter, somebody you'd want out front in a big fight." He was a captain of militia in his late twenties at Fort Orange, a position of considerable authority. He held the same post at what was originally called Wiltwyck ("wild place") on the banks of the Esopus Creek.

Chambers, an Englishman—some say Irish—was bilingual, fluent in both English and Dutch. Through trading with Native Americans around Fort Orange and Esopus, he was also familiar with their various dialects.

What the first settlers found at Esopus, Dietz said at his lecture, was fertile, cleared land along the creek with deep topsoil. Native Americans who had farmed the land for generations were willing to sell it to settlers. Chambers engaged local tribesmen to help him farm the land.

Chambers arrived in New Netherlands in 1642 at about the age of 20 where he worked as a carpenter and farmer. In 1646, he signed a five-year lease for a farm near present-day Troy in Rensselaerswyck. Two years later, he married wealthy widow Margriet Hendricks, a 28-year-old Dutch woman with four young children. Chambers, who twice married widows, never had children of his own.

After purchasing land from the natives, the settlers began occupying Wiltwyck in 1653, probably along the Esopus Creek. Amid increasing conflicts with Native Americans, the first Esopus Stockade was erected in 1658 under an agreement with New Netherland Governor Peter Stuyvesant. Chambers was a signer of that document.

Chambers's practice of paying his native workers with liquor may have been a factor in the first Esopus Indian War in 1659, when settlers fired on boisterous warriors. Chambers was one of 13 colonists captured, but was exchanged for a native prisoner. Stuyvesant sent a dozen Native Americans into slavery in Curaçao.

Chambers was instrumental in the founding of the Old Dutch Church. A lifelong supporter—he contributed generously to the construction of the church, the minister's house and a school—he was not a member until two years before his death. His first wife, who died in 1680, was an Old Dutch founder.

Chambers was working in his fields when Esopus Indians attacked the Stockade in 1663,

Chambers spoke many Indian dialects and was accepted as a trading partner

launching the Second Esopus War. As captain of militia, he rallied the settlers bringing the village cannon to bear on the attackers, who fled.

Chambers's role in the English takeover of New Amsterdam in 1664 has been the subject of some speculation. A confidant of Dutch Governor Stuyvesant, Chambers is credited by Ford and Dietz for a smooth transition with the incoming English. English governors, in their turn, allowed Dutch traditions to continue for decades. Dutch was still being spoken in Old Dutch Church services late in the nineteenth century.

Chambers held numerous posts in what became Kingston, He was a court magistrate and surveyor general of highways. He apparently acted as an attorney in some disputes, including several involving Stuyvesant's son.

He was so respected by the English that Governor Francis Lovelace designated his land, which Chambers called Fox Hall, a manor. Chambers had virtually complete authority within his domain. His home, which no longer exists, may have been located on the grounds of the current Newcombe estate off North Manor Avenue.

Chambers married the widow of Old Dutch Pastor Laurenties Van Gaasbeek in 1681 and adopted her son Abraham. Abraham carried the Chambers name in order to inherit his step-father's estate, but after his death his children reverted to being Van Gaasbeeks.

Chambers, who had gotten involved in shipping between Kingston and New York City, built a home in Rondout believed to be located under what is now the Loughran Bridge the year he remarried. A Chambers Street named for him was wiped out by urban renewal in the 1960s.

Chambers was buried under a pear tree on his property with a headstone that read "16TC94." The pear tree was taken down in 1926 and replaced on the grounds of the Kingston Visitors Center in 2005. The remnants of a pear from this tree may be preserved in a jar in the Senate House Museum, the last organic connection to the celebrated founder. Chambers's remains were transferred to Montrepose Cemetery in 1850. His original tombstone is in the Senate House.

Dietz was asked after his lecture why Kingstonians should know or even care about a man dead almost 320 years.

"It's our history," he replied. "The people of Kingston should know what happened here. It's their heritage. Quite a few of the early families have descendents alive and living here today. They should know the history of their own family."

The original lecture was presented by author and historian Ted Dietz on August 17, 2012.

2.

General George H. Sharpe: Spy Master of the Civil War

D id a Union Army officer from Kingston save Confederate General Robert E. Lee from a trial for treason and possible death on the gallows? Walt Witkowski, a local historian and authority on the life of General George H. Sharpe, Ulysses Grant's chief of military intelligence during the Civil War, thinks so.

The story, as told by Witkowski, a retired schoolteacher, in the second of a series of local history lectures at the Senate House Museum in Kingston, is an intriguing one. Sharpe raised the 120th Ulster Regiment at the beginning of the war and was its colonel. He was later assigned as chief of military intelligence by Army of the

General George H. Sharp

Military intelligence: The role of Kingston's General George Sharpe in the Civil War

Potomac commander Joseph Hooker. Sharpe, a graduate of Kingston and Albany academies and a Yale-educated lawyer, served in a similar capacity for General George Gordon Meade and finally for Grant.

A brigadier general by then, Sharpe was at Appomattox for the surrender of Lee's Army of Northern Virginia in April 1865. One of the duties assigned to him was securing "paroles" for officers in the defeated army. A parole in that context was defined as a sworn, signed statement that the parolee would not carry arms against the national government and would obey all laws in whatever area he settled in after the war.

Witkowski said that Sharpe, out of respect and courtesy to Lee, did not ask the commander of the Confederate Army to sign a parole. But Lee, "perhaps with an eye to the future," said Witkowski, insisted on being paroled "as a member of the Army of Northern Virginia." Sharpe, after consulting with Grant, issued the necessary documents.

Several months later, a committee of Congress composed of radical Republicans hell-bent on revenge against the South raised the possibility of trying Confederate leaders, including Lee, for treason, a crime punishable by death. Lee produced his parole papers, but it took a threat by Grant to resign as general-in-chief of the army to convince the radicals to drop the treason idea.

Witkowski said his interest in Sharpe began when his father took him as an 11-year-old to the Senate House in Kingston to view artifacts from the general then on display.

The historical researcher's 80-minute lecture attracted about 50 people and was followed by a brief question-and-answer session. Given the time constraints—Witkowski was told to hold his lecture to an hour—the speaker concentrated on Sharpe's military service during the Civil War.

Sharpe, then 33, a Kingston lawyer and businessman, raised the regiment of some 900 men in only a few weeks, Witkowski said. They were assigned to guard duty for their 90-day enlistment in Maryland. The first upstate regiment to report for duty, it sailed from Rondout on August 22, 1861. "Our whole trip to New York City was an ovation," Sharpe recorded.

Assigned to General Dan Sickles's corps, the 120th participated in the bloody battles of Fredericksburg and Chancellorsville, both Confederate victories.

Sharpe was offered the position of chief of the Bureau of Military Information (BMI), described by Witkowski as the first all-source intelligence agency in history. "Their work was decisively positive for the Army of the Potomac," Witkowski said.

As chief Union spy, Sharpe gathered information from numerous sources, including the BMI's network of 70 spies, captured Confederates, Southern newspapers, army patrols, telegraph intercepts, letters and diaries. Sharpe's staff would collate and coordinate data, analyze it, and offer assessments to commanding officers. "General Sharpe was unique in his operations in that he told his commanders what it was, not what he thought they wanted to hear," Witkowski said.

Slaves, either escaped or captured by Union forces, were a key source of information for Sharpe's BMI. "Southerners had a very low opinion of the intelligence of slaves," Witkowski said. "They thought them ignorant and often spoke freely in front of them. Well, they certainly were not ignorant, and the information they gave was often very valuable and accurate."

Sharpe's spies were quick to pick up Lee's northward movement after Chancellorsville in May, toward what would culminate in the battle of Gettysburg July 1 through 3, 1863. Sharpe was able to identify 100 Southern regiments, their makeup and direction and later their order of battle at Gettysburg.

Sharpe's information was vital in allowing the Army of the Potomac first to shield Washington from Lee's army and then to outrace it north into Pennsylvania and to assume commanding positions on the heights surrounding Gettysburg.

Sharpe's spies played another decisive role at Gettysburg, Witkowski said. After the second day of heavy casualties, Meade called a council of war with his officers "to decide wither to stay or go." At that council, Sharpe reported that Lee had left only one uncommitted unit, Pickett's division of Virginians. "We got 'em licked!" an officer shouted. Next day, Pickett's force was decimated in a frontal attack on the Union center. So accurate was Sharpe's intelligence regarding the Army of Northern Virginia in its chaotic final days that it appeared the spy in some respects knew more about the army than its commander.

Col. George Henry Sharpe sits at far left with other members of his "Bureau of Military Information," John C. Babcock, unidentified officer, and Lt. Col. John McEntee, 1864.

At Appomattox, Lee asked Grant for rations for his starving forces. Grant asked him how much he needed. Lee said rations for about 25,000 men. Sharpe corrected him. His intelligence had suggested a figure closer to 28,000, Witkowski said, a figure subsequently confirmed by the rations consumed.

While Witkowski's research indicates Sharpe was present in the McLean House at Appomattox where the surrender was signed, historical accounts vary. It is known that Sharpe purchased a pair of candlestick holders for ten dollars as souvenirs from the owner of the home. Sharpe later displayed the candlesticks at his home on Albany Avenue in Kingston. They were donated to the Senate House Museum with other memorabilia after his death in 1900.

Sharpe's post-war years were productive and prosperous. He was elected to the New York State Assembly in 1879 and served a term as speaker in 1881–82. He led the investigation that resulted in numerous convictions of the Boss Tweed Ring in the early 1870s.

Sharpe was a friend and confidant of Generals Grant and Sherman and of President Chester Arthur, whom he nominated for Vice President at the 1880 national Republican convention. All stayed at his home, called "The Orchard." The house was moved 200 feet to the west to make room for the Governor Clinton Hotel in 1924 and was demolished in the 1960s.

Sharpe remained active in veterans' organizations for the rest of his life, often holding leadership positions. In later years, Sharpe carried a cane engraved with the names of the officers from his regiment who had lost their lives in the war. In 1896, Sharpe raised a statue, "Daughter of the Regiment," to his men in the churchyard of the Old Dutch Church in Kingston, where he was a parishioner. "He never forgot his men," Witkowski said.

Sharpe and his wife, a Hasbrouck, had two children. Their son was a county judge in Kingston. Sharpe died at his daughter's home in New York City. Sharpe was buried with full military honors in Wiltwyck Cemetery. Lieutenant Colonel John Tappen of Kingston, his wartime aide, is buried nearby. The Sharp burial ground on Albany Avenue is named for an unrelated family.

And the candlesticks that had inspired Witkowski as an 11-year-old? "Now they're stored in a box at Peeble's Island [New York State historical research headquarters near Albany], never more to inspire an 11-year-old boy," Witkowski responded.

During the question-and-answer session, a member of the audience helped assuage the speaker's lament. "I was at Appomattox last year," she said. "The curator told us those candlestick holders are on permanent loan [and display] at the Smithsonian."

The original lecture was presented by historian Walter Witkowski on September 23, 2012.

3.

Alton B. Parker: The American Presidency's Gentleman Candidate

E ven a would-be Boswell might be challenged to write a biography on the life of Ulster's "colorless" Alton B. Parker, losing Democratic presidential candidate against Teddy Roosevelt in 1904. Parker was no Samuel Johnson.

"He was a gray, colorless man," Parker lecturer John Wadlin told an audience of about 50 attendees in the third installment of a five-part series on "Kingston's Buried (historical) Treasures" at the Senate House Museum. Wadlin, 69, a Kingston attorney and a Parker scholar, said he was considering writing the gray man's biography. Wadlin observed that Parker (1852–1926) is the only major party presidential candidate about whom a biography has not been written.

Alton B. Parker

Based on Wadlin's one-hour presentation, which included about 15 minutes of questions and answers, there wasn't much to write about Parker's presidential bid. Parker was nominated by Democrats in St. Louis in 1904 after turning back a challenge by publisher William Randolph Hearst. At the time

The Man Who Would Be King

Parker was Chief Judge of the New York State Court of Appeals, a position he resigned at the end of July that year to campaign for the presidency from his front porch in Esopus.

"To be positive, it was a very nice front porch," said Commissioner of Jurors Paul O'Neill to titters from the audience. Parker's running mate, 81-year-old Henry Davis of West Virginia, rarely left his home state, according to Wadlin, "perhaps because of his age."

Wadlin noted that Parker caused a stir shortly after being nominated by refusing to comment on one of the most controversial topics of the day, the gold standard. Besieged by reporters at his Rosemont home in Esopus, he finally relented by sending a telegram to the convention stating his support for what amounted to easy money. (Roosevelt took the same position.) He also told the convention if they didn't agree with his views they could nominate someone else. Citing his "courage," the party stuck with its nominee, Wadlin said.

Parker did venture as far as New York City a few weeks before Election Day to visit Democratic campaign headquarters. "Some people there didn't know who he was," Wadlin said.

On Election Day, Wadlin said Parker voted in Kingston and then went to his dentist. Parker's October charges of corruption in the Roosevelt administration were effectively blunted by the incumbent. "Prove it," Roosevelt said.

The results were a landslide. In the electoral vote Roosevelt carried 32 of 45 states, including Missouri. Parker took 38 percent of the popular vote, carrying only the Solid South. Roosevelt got 56 percent and Progressive Eugene Debs about 3 percent. Parker was thumped in his home state of New York by 175,000 votes (44 percent).

Parker was a distinguished lawyer and jurist, Wadlin said. Appointed a surrogate judge at the age of 25 in 1877 by a governor he had supported in the last election, Parker went on to serve as a Supreme Court judge and Chief Judge of the Court of Appeals, the latter position in his day a statewide elected office.

He is most noted for a decision on a case involving rights of privacy. A flower company had used a young woman's image on its flower bags without her knowledge and she sued for invasion of privacy, Wadlin said. The plaintiff prevailed in lower courts, but the Court of Appeals deadlocked at 3–3. As presiding judge, Parker cast the deciding vote against the plaintiff, ruling that under New York law there were no rights to privacy and that courts were not empowered to make law. Nonetheless, he urged the legislature to consider such laws, which were adopted shortly after. In modern parlance, he would have been considered a strict constructionist.

Winnisook Lake

Parker, a native of Cortland and a founding partner in the Winnisook Lodge in Big Indian, attended the 1908 and 1912 Democratic conventions as a delegate from New York. His ambition, Wadlin said, to be named a U.S. Supreme Court Judge was thwarted by philosophical differences with President Woodrow Wilson. Wadlin characterized Parker as "the last of the Gilded Age presidential candidates," while Wilson presented himself as a progressive.

Parker's focus on his lucrative New York City–based legal practice after the 1904 election made him a wealthy man. He died in 1926, willing Rosemont to his daughter and her family. There are no known descendants residing in the area.

The original lecture was presented by attorney John Wadlin on October 19, 2012.

4.

Sojourner Truth: Ulster County's Voice of Freedom

Sojourner Truth

One of the controversies over the proposed Dwight Eisenhower memorial in Washington was the monument committee's plan to depict Ike before he became a general and president—as a Kansas farm boy. The committee charged with creating a statue of abolitionist icon Sojourner Truth faced similar issues, ultimately deciding on an image closer to her roots in Ulster County as a girl born into slavery rather than her later fame as traveler, lecturer and abolitionist.

The "Daughter of Esopus" statue to be dedicated late next spring at the site of the former Town Hall on Broadway in Port Ewen will depict Truth as an 11-year-old girl. At that point in her life, Truth, known as Isabella, was owned by farmer John Dumont of West Park (then part of New Paltz) who had purchased her for $175. Born a slave about 1797 on the Hardenburgh farm in Rifton, Truth was the youngest of 13 siblings, none of whom she ever knew. Her language, according to lecturer and County Historian Anne

Her Aim Was Truth

Gordon of Port Ewen, was "low Dutch," all but incomprehensible to English ears. She learned English, but always retained her Dutch accent. Gordon was the most recent speaker in the series "Kingston's Buried Treasures" at the Senate House Museum.

By age 11, Truth had already been sold twice. Severely beaten at times—she would show the scars at lectures later in life—she worked for farmers, one of whom taught her English, and a tavern owner in Port Ewen under conditions that are almost unimaginable today. She was forced into marriage at about the age of 20; the union produced a son, Peter, and three daughters. A hard worker, she was said to be "worth the price of two men," according to Gordon.

"As a young slave, she walked these roads of Esopus. That's how we wanted to depict her," Gordon told an audience of about 65 persons at the Senate House Museum. Truth left the Hudson Valley for New York City to pursue Methodist missionary work among the poor and African Americans in 1829, never, apparently, to return. She died in 1883 and is buried in Battle Creek, Michigan. Gordon said Truth has about 400 descendants, divided between Battle Creek and California.

Funding for the $91,000 five-foot bronze sculpture was derived largely through a grant secured by Assemblyman Kevin Cahill, D-Kingston, whose 101st District includes Esopus. "It was a lot of money and it was difficult raising, all things considered," Gordon said. "We went to Assemblyman Cahill and I was immediately impressed by his unquestionable acceptance of honoring Sojourner Truth in the town where she lived. He gets it." Gordon is a former Democratic legislator from Esopus.

New Paltz sculptor Trina Greene, interviewed after Gordon's Sojourner Truth lecture, said she gave a great deal of study and thought to the image she and the committee wanted to present.

"I imagined she was kind of gangly at that age," Greene said of Truth, who in maturity was an imposing figure by nineteenth-century standards, well over six feet tall. Greene said she used as models images from a 1970s photo book authored by onetime Nazi propagandist Leni Riefenstahl on West African natives of the Kau tribe, and two New Paltz 11-year-olds—her granddaughter Lindsay Greene and Lindsay's classmate, Allie Defoe. Greene said many of the early American slaves were captured in West Africa. The Kau people she studied, she said, "were very tall and beautiful."

Greene said she also attempted to capture some of what she believed was the character of an 11-year-old Sojourner Truth, an illiterate child approaching womanhood who had suffered many of the horrors and degradations of slavery but one with an inner determination and pride she hid from her masters, a "sense of her true grit and sweetness." Truth's

childhood qualities of character would be demonstrated later in life as an abolitionist and as an early advocate of women's rights.

"She really was America's voice of freedom, both racial and gender," said County Commissioner of Jurors Paul O'Neill, moderator for the continuing lecture series called "Kingston's Buried Treasures."

After legally and literally "walking to freedom" in 1826, she gained early fame in 1828 by suing her master in Ulster County Court for the return of her son, Peter. Peter later became a sailor on a whaling boat out of New Bedford, Massachusetts, and was apparently lost at sea.

Truth met Abraham Lincoln during the Civil War. Reports of their conversation, which might have been apocryphal, went something like this, Gordon told her audience:

"I never heard of you before you were president," said Truth.

"But I've heard of you," Lincoln replied.

The original lecture was presented by Ulster County Historian Anne Gordon on November 16, 2012.

Photo on Left: Commemorative statue of Sojourner Truth as a girl. Port Ewen, New York

5.

Thomas Cornell: Vanderbilt of the Rondout

The wealthiest man in town around the time of the founding of Kingston as a city in 1872, Thomas Cornell owned fleets of boats that dominated Hudson River passenger and freight trade. He also owned railroads that carried thousands of tourists, two banks and a daily newspaper. He made fortunes in the bluestone and cement industries.

"He was such a dominant force in this city, on this river, in this region, but today he's relatively unknown," said Ulster County Commissioner of Jurors Paul O'Neill in introducing Stuart Murray, the author of a biography on Cornell, at the monthly historical series, "Kingston's

Thomas Cornell

Kingston's Robber Baron

Buried Treasures." The purpose of the series is to revive interest in the city's heritage.

Cornell (1814–1890) was born in White Plains and came to Rondout in 1837. He soon parlayed ownership of a small Hudson River sloop into the largest steamboat company in the country.

Murray detailed how Cornell, from the most modest beginnings, rose to be admired as "the Vanderbilt of the Rondout" through a combination of timing, geography, hard work, fierce determination and the luck of living in an age of unfettered capitalism. The Cornell Steamboat Company, headquartered

The Rondout, the source of an empire

at the foot of Broadway on the Rondout, established dominance on the Hudson in an era when the D&H Canal was shipping millions of tons of coal from Pennsylvania to Rondout for transit to New York. Brickyards up and down the Hudson were helping build the nation's largest city. The bluestone and cement industries were booming, and local agriculture was feeding the masses. One of Cornell's boats once transported 36,000 baskets of raspberries from Marlborough, according to Murray.

While Cornell's business interests ranged beyond the horizon, he had enormous power in his adopted home town. At its height near the end of the nineteenth century, the Cornell Steamboat Company was the city's largest employer, with more than 400 workers.

Cornell Street in Kingston is named for him—but not Cornell University in Ithaca, founded by Cornell's cousin, Ezra. A firehouse on Abeel Street carried his name. To serve his customers, Cornell owned the Grand Hotel in Highmount. His ship *Manhattan* transported the first Ulster County soldiers to the Civil War and served the North throughout the conflict. More famously, he owned the *Mary Powell*, the Hudson's most illustrious side-wheeler. At Kingston Point, passengers disembarked from Cornell-owned steamboats on one side of a two-story platform and boarded a Cornell-owned railroad on the other.

In politics, Cornell was a staunch "Lincoln" Republican. Twice congressman from Ulster County, he was a delegate to every Republican national convention from 1864 to 1888.

Known as "The Major" for his service in the state militia, Cornell and his family lived

The Mary Powell, Queen of the Hudson

in a mansion overlooking the Rondout and the Hudson at the corner of Wurts and Spring Streets, later occupied by State Senator Jacob Rice. The building was torn down in 1942. The vacant lot remains guarded by a stone wall erected in Cornell's time. The adjacent Cornell Park is named for him.

Cornell and his wife had four children; the two boys and one girl died in childhood. His surviving daughter married Samuel Decker Coykendall, who succeeded his father-in-law and considerably enhanced the business.

Coykendall, who died in 1913, had six children, only one of whom, a daughter, had children. According to Kingston historian Edwin Ford, there are no Cornell or Coykendall descendants living in the area. The founder and his heirs are buried in Montrepose Cemetery in Kingston. The Cornell Steamboat Company was founded in

Thomas Cornell House

1837 and endured until 1963, under the direction of S.D. Coykendall's heirs.

Murray, the author of more than a dozen books, said he developed an interest in steamboats as a child living in Port Ewen. He collaborated on the Cornell book, published by Purple Mountain Press in 2001, with renowned Hudson River steamboat authorities Roger Mabie, William D. Thomas and Bill Spangenberger, last president of the Cornell Steamboat Company. Murray's lecture, like his book, is a reminder of the rich industrial and transportation heritage of Kingston.

The original lecture was presented by author Stuart Murray on December 14, 2012.

6.

George Fletcher Chandler: The Founder of the New York State Police

Col. George Fletcher Chandler

How a Kingston Physician Became the Founder of the New York State Police

Though he was a doctor, scholar, violinist, professor, soldier and cavalryman, George Fletcher Chandler is best known by every trooper as the founder of the New York State Police. Colonel Chandler—he served briefly in the Army Medical Corps as an administrator in World War II and preferred the title "colonel" to that of doctor or superintendent—owed that fame to a casual conversation with the governor of the state in April 1917.

As state police Major Robin Benziger, Director of Training at the NYS Trooper Academy in Albany, told her audience at the recent installment of the "Kingston's Buried (historical) Treasures" series at the Senate House, Chandler, then a practicing physician in Kingston, was called to Albany to discuss Governor Charles Whitman's idea of a state police force to patrol rural New York.

Daring Men and Well-bred Horses

Whitman and Chandler had been classmates at Columbia University in New York City some 35 years previous, where Chandler had studied medicine and Whitman law. The two had talked only occasionally over the years, so Benziger said Chandler was "quite surprised" by the governor's invitation for him to head the force.

"They talked over old times for a while, and then the governor asked Dr. Chandler for his views on a state police force," Benziger told her audience. Chandler had been an officer in the National Guard for about ten years, where he had been a range instructor and an equestrian. He had attended the Army service school in 1909 and participated in the hunt for Pancho Villa in Mexico in 1916, at around the same time reformers Katherine Mayo and Moyca Newell had begun lobbying the legislature for a state police force. (The first trooper training camp at a National Guard center in Manlius was named Newayo for the pair.) The idea met with fierce opposition from unions and other police agencies, Benziger said. A bill establishing the force and allocating $500,000 to get it going passed the legislature by a single vote.

According to Benziger, the governor turned to the window after about two hours of discussion with Chandler and exclaimed, "I have the man. And it is you!"

Chandler replied that he wasn't interested, as he knew little about police work. A few days later, Whitman invited Chandler to a private luncheon with former President Teddy

Colonel Chandler's early recruits

Roosevelt, who at that point was attempting to raise a cavalry regiment to fight the Germans in France. Roosevelt, then 58, wanted to recruit Chandler, 44, as his chief of cavalry, but President Woodrow Wilson, one of Roosevelt's opponents in the 1912 election and a frequent target of his pointed criticism, nixed the idea of latter-day Rough Riders. What was exactly said at that lunch is lost to history, but it undoubtedly influenced Chandler's change of heart. Chandler was formally appointed the first state police superintendent on May 2, 1917, less than a month after the United States declared war on Germany.

The Gray Rider monument in front of the New York State Police Academy

Chandler briefly served in the army in 1918–19 as a medical officer. He returned to New York to find a new governor bent on disbanding the force. In June of that year, Chandler convinced Governor Al Smith that his state police could become the best police force in the nation. Smith relented and became an avid supporter.

Born in the western New York hamlet of Clyde, Chandler was a prodigy on the violin, an instrument he played all his life. He attended Syracuse University on a music scholarship and graduated from Columbia Medical College in 1895. He married and moved to Kingston in 1905. The family lived on East Chestnut Street. He had two sons.

Chandler's busy medical practice touched many lives. "He removed the tonsils of my two brothers," City Historian Edwin Ford, 94, said after Benziger's lecture.

"He was a true Renaissance man, enormously creative, with a rare gift for organization," Benziger told her audience of about 60 persons.

Based on his own military experience, Chandler saw the state police as a semi-military organization. As a physician he personally examined every one of the first 232 recruits for the force. Given the high standards set by the new superintendent, pickings were slim. Some 50 National Guardsmen mounted patrol soldiers had to be recruited to fill the ranks. Chandler wanted unmarried "daring" men between the ages of 21 and 35, slender but strong, weighing between 145 and 165 pounds.

Chandler had a hand in everything from curriculum to uniform design, from weaponry to the chain of command. He personally selected 243 Morgan horses from Missouri for trooper mounts and later made arrangements with local farmers to breed horses for his men. His wife's affection for the color purple was incorporated in the uniforms.

New York State Police Troopers today

Police officers as public servants

In a remarkably short period, Chandler recruited, trained, wrote service manuals and equipped his fledgling force. Chandler had a keen eye for detail, as evidenced by his designation of a gray uniform for troopers, equally composed of black and white threads, signifying the presence of good and evil in all things. He ordered 50 Stetson hats from Philadelphia and personally cut them into the distinctive design troopers wear to this day.

By the time the first superintendent left after seven years, the force numbered over 700 men. Women, recruited beginning in 1973, now number about 10 percent of the 4,500-member state police force. The Bureau of Criminal Investigation (BCI) was founded in the early 1930s, ten years after Chandler left.

Chandler, whose stern visage in period photos belied his "terrific sense of humor," according to Benziger, saw his force first in terms of public service and then as police officers. His motto was: "A policeman is only a citizen who has chosen to be a servant of the public, one having no more or no less rights than any other citizen." This statement is still memorized by every recruit. Chandler expected his men, who were often the only police presence in a wide rural area, to follow the best professional examples of doctors, lawyers and clergymen.

He coined another trooper motto: "Obedience to the law is liberty."

Chandler left the troopers in 1923, telling Smith his work was done and the department was in good hands. He returned to Kingston, where he practiced medicine until 1932, retiring at age 60 as he had planned when he started his career. He and his second wife traveled the world thereafter.

As a pioneer and innovator in police work and organization, Chandler was frequently called on to lecture or speak on law-enforcement topics. He continued to play the violin in retirement and on occasion conducted symphony orchestras.

Chandler lived his last years in the Governor Clinton Hotel in Kingston. He died in a nursing home in 1964 and ordered his ashes cast at Glenerie Falls south of Saugerties, where an earlier state police station had been located.

In the mid-1950s, the Thruway Authority named the connecting link between Kingston and the Thruway traffic circle, the shortest Interstate highway in America, after Chandler. Shortly after he died, the county legislature dedicated a monument to Chandler that stands at the entrance of what was then the new county office building in Kingston.

The original lecture was presented by New York State Police Major Robin Benziger on January 18, 2013.

Troopers first set out on horseback, working independently to cover the entire state during 30 day tours of duty

7.

Ezra Fitch: Founder of Abercrombie & Fitch

They came from all over to hear city historian Edwin Ford lecture on Ezra Fitch, one of Kingston's more obscure "buried treasures." Ford, city historian for some 30 years, is much admired for his encyclopedic knowledge and incisive understanding of Kingston history.

Introduced by "Buried Treasures" series master of ceremonies Paul O'Neill, tongue in cheek, as "our only lecturer who has actually lived in the lifetime of his subject," the 94-year-old Ford, seated at the podium, responded, "Pardon me for sitting, but I don't think I could stand for a four-hour lecture." The overflow crowd, knowing that the

Ezra Fitch

"Buried Treasures" lectures at the Senate House Museum on Fair Street are strictly limited to one hour, chuckled. Ford, after offering a wealth of information, finished 13 minutes ahead of schedule.

From Fair Street to Madison Avenue—Kingston's Outfitter to the World

Even for a local historian of Ford's sagacity, Ezra Fitch (1865–1930) may have been a challenge. He lived in Kingston for only about six years, departing for New York City in 1900 to partner with small-time sporting goods purveyor and outfitter David

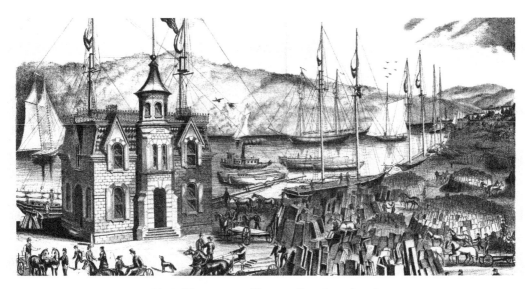

Fitch Bluestone offices at Rondout Creek

Abercrombie. Fitch was born and raised in Coxsackie and attended law school at New York University.

Before a standing-room crowd of about 80 persons. Ford devoted about half his lecture to Fitch's namesake, his grandfather Ezra Fitch, the Kingston bluestone magnate. "You're lucky tonight there were two Ezra Fitches," Ford told his audience. "I debated which one to talk about first." He chose chronological order.

The first Fitch came to Kingston in 1828 and formed a partnership to ship bluestone, a booming industry in the Sawkill area, up and down the Hudson River. The partners settled in what was then known as Twaalfskill Landing at the foot of Wilbur Avenue because, Ford said, the Broadway hill which ends at the Rondout Creek was too steep for heavy loads of bluestone.

The first Ezra, apparently sentimental about Christmas, built a riverboat called *The Santa Claus* and later a hotel for boatmen called the Santa Claus Hotel across from the Fitch shipping office. It was demolished in the 1970s and replaced by a private home built by the Lawlis family. Family patriarch James Berardi acquired and renovated the long-vacant Fitch bluestone office across the street for a private residence at about the same time. Ford said he had been one of "several thousand" persons who attended an open house at the Fitch-Berardi residence.

The elder Ezra retired in 1854 after selling his steamer to Thomas Cornell, the subject of a previous lecture. His nephew built the distinctive Victorian Fitch shipping office in 1870. Constructed from bluestone at a cost of $10,000, Ford said it was called the finest office building in Ulster County in its day. Its architect, J.A. Wood of Poughkeepsie, designed the Baptist church on Albany Avenue and a renovation of St. Joseph's Catholic Church on Main Street.

By 1890, the boom years of bluestone construction were over.

Ford said he traced the Fitch name back to the English King Edward I in 1292, "200 years before Columbus." The family immigrated to Connecticut in 1633.

Young Ezra Fitch's father died in 1888, after which the son lived for a period in California. He returned to study law in 1892 in New York City, where he made the acquaintance of David Abercrombie, who that year opened a small sporting goods and apparel store on South Street in lower Manhattan.

Fitch was admitted to the bar in 1895 and began the practice of law in Kingston with James Jenkins. The partners had a law office in a building (demolished in the 1960s) next door to the present county office building. He married Sarah Huntington Sturges of Stone Ridge in 1897. They lived in a large home at the corner of Fair Street and Maiden Lane, about 100 yards from his office.

The law partners dabbled in real estate, building several structures in Kingston. The most notable was the Huntington Hotel at 23 Pearl Street, later torn down for a parking lot for the adjacent United Methodist Church.

Fitch was an avid outdoorsman, yachtsman, National Guardsman, golfer and crack rifle shot. He apparently did business with Abercrombie, who catered to an exclusive clientele. Ford said Fitch belonged to Twaalfskill Golf Club and the Kingston Masonic Lodge. He was a member of the Ulster County Bar Association.

Bored with the law, Fitch moved to New York City in 1900 and formed a partnership with Abercrombie. The firm was renamed Abercrombie & Fitch in 1904.

The partners clashed. Abercrombie resisted Fitch's efforts to expand their market, feeling it would cheapen their brand. Ford recounted how Fitch advocated for a mail-order business (like Sears Roebuck and Montgomery Ward and other major retailers). The mail-order catalog he launched (as sole owner) in 1909 "almost broke the company," Ford said, though it produced enormous sales.

In 1907, the same year Abercrombie sold out to Fitch, the firm moved to a twelve-story building on Madison Avenue, advertised as the largest store of its kind in the world. "The clerks were rugged outdoorsmen who would rather talk about their specialties to their customers than sell anything," Ford said. "Selling was only performed at the customer's insistence, kind of like the big-box stores of today."

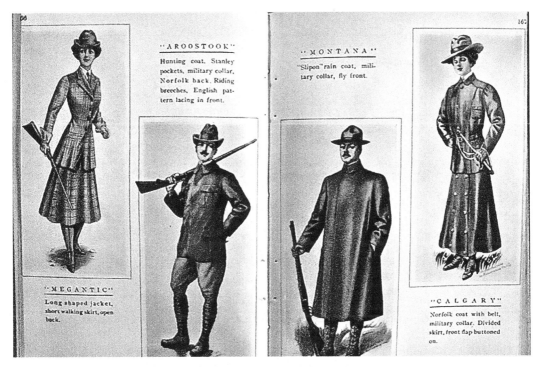

Early Abercrombie & Fitch catalogue

The store featured a rifle range in the cellar and a pond on the roof so fishermen could test their gear. Large stuffed animals and fish abounded. "Goods were displayed in outdoor, realistic settings, not hidden on shelves in warehouses," Ford said.

The company was generations ahead of its time in marketing. It publicized the names of its more famous customers, who included several presidents, famous actors, aviators and at least one composer. Cole Porter bought his evening clothes from A&F. Ford said Charles Lindbergh bought outfits for his historic flight to Paris in 1927 from Abercrombie & Fitch.

"Did he wear any underwear?" Ford mused. "Probably not. He took off in a plane loaded with gasoline that barely got off the ground. Weight was an issue."

Abercrombie & Fitch is credited with launching the Mahjong craze in America in 1920.

Fitch retired from business in 1928 and died on his yacht off Santa Barbara, California, in 1930. According to Ford there are no living Fitch descendants in the area.

Abercrombie & Fitch, calling itself "the greatest sporting-goods store in the world," eventually went bankrupt in the 1970s. It was purchased for $1.5 million in 1978, revived, and was sold again for $47 million to publicly traded Limited Brands (Victoria's Secret and other big chains) in 1988. Sales doubled to $165 million in 1994. Revenues now exceed $3.5 billion in more than 1000 stores across the world.

There were growing pains, Ford noted. In hewing to Abercrombie's elitist tradition, the enterprise was accused of racism (hiring only white males), sexism and what one woman in the audience called "abominably bad taste" in offering padded bikinis for five-year-old girls.

Ford himself cringed when recounting some company abuses, like a shirt for girls, quickly withdrawn, that read, "If you have two of these, you don't need brains."

"If Ezra knew what they were selling now, he would be very upset," the historian deadpanned.

The original lecture was presented by Kingston City Historian Edwin Ford on February 15, 2013.

8.

John Vanderlyn:
Painter of a Nation

O nce one of America's renowned artists, John Vanderlyn died a destitute old man in a rundown hotel in 1852, only two blocks away from where he was born two years before the British burned Kingston.

His story is one of precocious talent displayed at an early age, association with leading figures of his day, a quest for fortune and fame and for promoting the study of classic art. As Rosendale graphic artist Joseph Tantillo told an audience at the eighth installment of "Kingston's Buried Treasures" in the Vanderlyn Gallery of the Senate House Museum, Vanderlyn,

John Vanderlyn, self portrait - 1800

who spent much of his life studying and working in Europe, was a man out of step with his countrymen.

Vanderlyn was a neo-classicist who painted historic panoramas at a time when the Hudson River School of art began to celebrate the expansion of America through landscapes. Despite celebrated landscapes like one of

Out of Step—A Flawed Genius

Panoramic View of the Palace and Gardens of Versailles - 1814–18

Niagara Falls, Vanderlyn is not associated with the school.

Thomas Jefferson bought one of the earliest prints of Vanderlyn's painting of the iconic falls. The artist's panorama of Versailles is on display at the Metropolitan Museum of Art in New York. His sketches for the painting are in the collection of the Senate House Museum, which has the largest collections of his work.

"I don't know if Vanderlyn and Thomas Cole (founder of the Hudson River School) knew each other, but they certainly had very different views of art," Tantillo said. "The Hudson River School had a lot to do with natural beauty, with God's blessings on this new land, a sort of nationalism. Vanderlyn did not see art that way. He would have looked at it as not that interesting. He liked mythology, historic painting, classic art. Things of man that were refined would have much more value to him."

Vanderlyn achieved considerable fame, if not fortune, in his more than 50-year career. His painting of *The Landing of Columbus* hangs in the Capitol Rotunda in Washington and has been featured on U.S. currency and stamps. He was the first to paint Niagara Falls (in 1801). His portraits of presidents from Washington to Taylor hang in famous galleries.

But Vanderlyn's (1846) painstaking painting of Columbus's landing, which some said was crafted by an assistant, was dismissed by one critic as "hardly more than respectable."

Landing of Columbus - 1839–46

His present reputation is that he was "a prominent regional artist" whose works rarely appear on the market.

Vanderlyn was born in October 1775 near the corner of Wall and John Streets, one of five children of Nicholas and Sara (Tappen) Vanderlyn. His grandfather, Peter Vanderlyn, was a native of Holland and a well-known artist.

The family was burned out of its home by the British in 1777, two years after Vanderlyn's birth. The house was never rebuilt, and the family lived in a lean-to on the property. Vanderlyn, who attended Kingston Academy, showed artistic talent as a child and by age 16 was studying art at the Columbia Academy of Art in New York City and working in an art-supply house. Tantillo said

1795 portrait of Aaron Burr

Vanderlyn met famed portrait painter Gilbert Stuart when the latter came to the art store to frame a portrait of Aaron Burr he had recently completed. Vanderlyn asked if he could copy the painting, a common practice for art students.

In 1795, Peter Van Gaasbeeck of Kingston purchased the painting and presented it to Burr. Impressed by the youngster's talent, Burr sent Vanderlyn to study under Stuart, where he painted copies of Stuart's famous patrons, among them George Washington (depicted on the dollar bill). Burr sent him to Paris in 1796 where Vanderlyn learned, among other disciplines, miniature portraiture. His dime-sized "eye of Theodosia Burr" is one of his more famous works. The original is in the Senate House gallery. He was the first American artist to study in Paris rather than London.

Rumors of romance between Theodosia and Vanderlyn were probably unfounded, Tantillo said, because of the eight-year difference in their ages and Burr's ambition to marry his only daughter into the Southern aristocracy. She was lost at sea in 1813.

As described by Tantillo, Vanderlyn seemed a man of contradiction and conflict, argumentative and stubborn in his beliefs. "He was depicted as very bitter and unpleasant, a prima donna with a bad disposition," Tantillo said. "It was said that strong beer made him easier to deal with."

Vanderlyn first attracted attention for his portrait painting. According to Tantillo, he became one of the most admired portrait painters of his day but did so only to pay his

**Caius Marius Amid the Ruins
of Carthage - 1808**

bills. "You could see it [his popularity] in his commissions—presidents, famous figures—right up to the end of his life when he painted President Zachary Taylor [in 1850]," Tantillo said.

His early patron was Aaron Burr, then a United States senator from New York. Burr recognized Vanderlyn's talent and sent him to France to study art in 1796. Vanderlyn's fortunes rose, and apparently fell, with Burr's. After Burr's infamous duel with Alexander Hamilton in 1804 and his subsequent trial and acquittal for treason, Burr fled to Paris, where Tantillo said he for a time was supported by Vanderlyn.

In 1808, Vanderlyn won a gold medal, presented by Napoleon, for his painting of *Caius Marius Amid the Ruins of Carthage*. Some saw the work as an allegory of Burr's downfall. Vanderlyn's refusal to sell the painting to the emperor was a footnote that brought murmurs from Tantillo's audience.

While seeking fortune through his work, Vanderlyn seemed to have little aptitude or interest in the financial side of his profession. At times, Tantillo said, his teenaged nephew, John Vanderlyn II (the artist never married), handled his financial transactions. The result was the older man's continuous debt and eventual destitution. It is recorded that Vanderlyn had to borrow money to transport his baggage from Rondout Landing in the summer of 1852 to the Kingston Hotel on Crown Street, where he died that September. The remaining parts of the building were demolished in the 1980s to expand a parking lot. Vanderlyn is buried in Wiltwyck Cemetery beneath a monument donated by admirers. While the name is common to this area, there are no known descendants of the artist.

The original lecture was presented by artist and historian Joe Tantillo on March 15, 2013.

9.

Ulster County Courthouse: Birthplace of New York State

Where were the gallows?"

That's the question Ulster County Commissioner of Jurors Paul O'Neill says he gets most frequently from visitors to Ulster County's historic courthouse in Kingston. Speculation about the gallows hang around the longest, ranging from a back room in the jail, now the grand jury room, to under the cupola.

"There were never any gallows in the building," O'Neill told his audience at the ninth installment of the "Kingston's Buried Treasures" series at the Senate House Museum. "I've been up in the tower and there's no way they could have carried a body down from there."

Ulster County Courthouse

Up until the mid-nineteenth century, condemned criminals were publicly hanged about 100 yards from the courthouse, near the corner of Wall and Pearl Streets, O'Neill said. "It was done publicly as a deterrent," he said. "Sadly, it was also entertainment for the crowds that gathered."

A Cornerstone of American History

In a less lethal form of public spectacle, prisoners held for minor crimes were placed in stocks on the courthouse lawn, there to suffer the

Gouverneur Morris, John Jay and Robert Livingston

ridicule of passers-by, some heaving rotten fruit and vegetables.

Inside the classic Federal-style building and on the plot of land on which it sits, justice has been meted out for almost 325 years by county and state supreme courts. Used as a community meeting place in its earliest years, O'Neill said the courthouse was where the New York State Constitution was debated and adopted in April 1777. The first reading was from its front steps.

General George Clinton was sworn in as the state's first governor in front of the courthouse. Gouverneur Morris, later a co-author of the preamble to the U.S. Constitution and writer of the famous phrase "We the people," appeared in the Ulster courthouse as a member of the state Constitutional Convention.

Kingstonians gathered in front of the courthouse in April 1861 to hear the news of the attack on Fort Sumter. Active recruiting of Union regiments began there.

Other justices of the Supreme Court who practiced at the courthouse included Henry Brockholst Livingston (not to be confused with the more prominent Chancellor

Gov. George Clinton

Robert Livingston), a member of the New York City branch of the family and John Jay's brother-in-law (1807–1823); Smith Thompson of Amenia (1823–1843), New York Chief Justice in his latter years; and Rufus Peckham of Albany, U.S. Supreme Court Justice (1896–1909), a notable supporter of big business.

Great moment in freedom

As the plaque in front of the building indicates, the courthouse is where Sojourner Truth, born a slave, argued successfully in 1828 for the freedom of her son, who was sent to the South as a slave. "The courthouse is the place where the people come to see justice done," O'Neill said. "It is the people's courthouse. It is our courthouse."

Sojourner Truth

Alton B. Parker of Esopus practiced at the courthouse before service on the state Supreme Court and as Chief Justice of the state Court of Appeals. He ran for president against Theodore Roosevelt in 1904. (He lost.)

Civil War General George Sharpe also practiced law at what is colloquially called "1818," mostly likely walking from his mansion at 1 Albany Avenue, since 1923 the site of the Governor Clinton Hotel. Ezra Fitch, partner and owner of Abercrombie & Fitch in the early part of the twentieth century, was another lawyer with roots in the county courthouse.

During the question-and-answer session following his 45-minute address, O'Neill, an attorney, was asked to speak to prominent trials held in the courthouse. "All trials are important," he said.

The original lecture was presented by Commissioner of Jurors Paul O'Neill on April 19, 2013.

A Chronology of the Ulster County Courthouse

The first courthouse was presumed to have been built some time after 1661 after the first extension of the original Stockade built in 1658. It served a joint purpose as "community house," minister's residence and courthouse. It was located at the intersection of Wall and John streets.

1683—The first stand-alone courthouse with jail was constructed at its present site.

1732—After years of repairs, new construction was authorized on a courthouse and jail. Courthouse construction didn't begin immediately due to difficulty in raising authorized tax levies for the jail from the towns.

1737—Fieldstone courthouse with cupola was under construction.

1777—The British burn the courthouse, destroying its interior, but the outer walls remain. Work begins on restoration. The building remains in service until 1816.

1816–1817—Building torn down and rebuilt on original foundation. Construction of a new courthouse and jail begins.

1818—New courthouse/jail complex is dedicated.

1834—Addition built to expand jail facilities.

1868—Addition to the western end for new jail.

1899—Last jail addition.

1972—County opens new jail on Golden Hill, "1818" abandoned as a jail. Three courtrooms created in jail space.

1990s—Extensive renovation of jail space and the rest of the building.

10.

Colonel George Pratt: Commander of the Ulster Guard

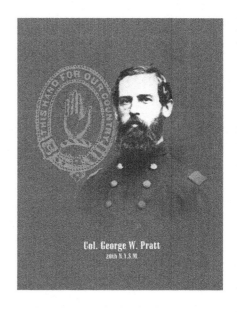

Col. George W. Pratt
20th N.Y.S.M.

S cion of immense wealth, author, historian and state senator before the age of 30, George Pratt seemed destined for greatness. The Civil War elevated him to a different kind of glory. Colonel George Pratt was mortally wounded while leading his men of the Ulster Guard against Stonewall Jackson's troops at the Second Battle of Bull Run in late August 1862. Pratt died less than two weeks later in Albany.

"He might have gone to great heights—governor, United States senator, maybe more," historian Walt Witkowski said of the remarkably accomplished leader killed in the early prime of his life. Witkowski was filling in for Pratt authority Seward Osborne of Krumville, who was unable to attend the scheduled lecture on Pratt, the tenth in a series called "Kingston's Buried Treasures."

A Fallen Hero in the War for the Union

It was Osborne who had suggested to Paul O'Neill, coordinator of the "Buried Treasures" series, that Pratt should be included. O'Neill said he didn't see the strong Kingston connection until he was told Pratt had lived near Kingston from 1857, in a home south of the city. Pratt, who wrote what is considered the definitive account of the Burning of Kingston, was a state senator representing Ulster and Greene counties and was a founder of the Ulster County Historical Society. The multi-talented Pratt also designed the distinctive "This Hand for My Country" emblem—based on the traditional banner of the original Ulster County in Ireland—of the 20th Ulster Guard.

Witkowski approached his subject with homage to Osborne. "Seward studied Colonel Pratt for 40 years," he said. "I had only three weeks to prepare."

"Almost all the material I will present is from Seward's extensive research," Witkowski told his audience at the Senate House Museum on Fair Street. "Osborne has written the only biography of Pratt and was instrumental in convincing the National Park Service to erect a plaque where Pratt was shot down at Second Manassas."

George Watson Pratt, the only son of wealthy industrialist and banker Zadock Pratt and his wife Abigail, was born in Schoharieville (later renamed Prattsville) in Greene County on

Zadock Pratt

April 18, 1830. Home-schooled in his early years, he was enrolled in the Poughkeepsie Collegiate (boarding) School at age 14. Pratt's father, colonel of the Greene County 28th Militia, encouraged his son's interest in military affairs.

Zadock Pratt was one of the major tanners in the Catskills. At age 16, George Pratt convinced his father that travel abroad would be educational and worthwhile for him. Pratt's journey took him to dozens of countries in Europe and the Mideast. He climbed Mount Vesuvius and the Great Pyramid in Egypt. Pratt, according to Witkowki, had a natural affinity for

languages, speaking half a dozen fluently. He also developed an interest in old books and manuscripts. In time, his personal library included more than 8,000 publications.

He returned home in 1849 but left the year after for another round of travel with his sister Julia. Wealthy traveling Americans were "accepted in the parlors of Europe" during the mid-nineteenth century, Witkowski explained. Pratt was able to meet and converse with leading figures of his time, with a particular interest in military science.

He returned to business in 1852, financed by his father, and was also elected a captain in his father's regiment. At age 23 he was New York State quartermaster for a year. He was a founder of the Military Association of New York, whose goal was to modernize the state's militias, and its first president.

George Pratt married Anna Tibbets of Albany in 1856. Their first child, George Seymour Pratt, was born a year later, and their second, Elizabeth Tibbets Pratt, in 1860.

In the autumn of 1857, the 27-year-old Pratt came to Kingston where he joined the uptown Masonic Lodge. Shortly thereafter he was elected colonel of the 20th NYS Militia,

The Ulster Guard

which had merged with the 28th Greene Militia. A Republican, he was elected state senator from Ulster-Greene in 1857, the youngest member of the Senate.

Named a vestryman of St. John's Episcopal Church in 1858, Pratt donated $1,000 to a church fund drive. His wife commissioned a stained-glass window in the church on Albany Avenue. (It was originally located on Wall Street between North Front and John streets. The church was dismantled stone by stone and moved to its present location in the mid-1820s.) In 1859, Pratt bought the 150-acre Atwood Farm in West Park for $36,000. The house, still standing, is located on the Marist Brothers property on the Hudson River.

While serving in the state Senate, Pratt was on the military affairs committee, which helped modernize state militias. He also voted to approve the charter of the Ulster County Savings Institution (later Ulster Savings Bank). He was a founder of the Ulster County Historical Society in 1859.

Using research from original British military records in London, Pratt wrote the history of the 1777 burning of Kingston in 1860, an account British authorities called "factual in every respect."

With war looming and several Southern states seceding following the election of Abraham Lincoln in 1860, Pratt met with officers of the 20th Regiment in mid-January. Governor Edwin Morgan had asked for 13,000 New York volunteers to meet the state's share of the president's call for 75,000 soldiers and sailors.

On April 28 Pratt swore in his regiment on Academy Green in Uptown Kingston. The regiment departed from Rondout by boat to New York City. On May 7, it became the first upstate New York regiment to go to war.

The regiment saw no combat during its 90 days in Federal service, but performed the important function of helping secure Baltimore, Witkowki said. At the beginning of the war, Maryland was considered a hotbed of Southern sympathies. Amid threats of assassination, Lincoln was smuggled in disguise through Baltimore on a special train in March 1861 for his inauguration. Had Maryland seceded, Washington would have been isolated behind Confederate lines.

The 20th was ordered home on July 3. Pratt, who apparently understood from his military training that it could be a long war, asked his men voluntarily to extend their enlistments for two years. About half did. Pratt then recruited another 450 men to bring the regiment up to full strength, about 950 men.

Pratt's family pleaded with him not to return to war. "You've done your job," his wife said. "I shall go again," he is recorded as saying. In October, the regiment returned to the war.

After wintering in quarters, the Army of the Potomac and Pratt's regiment resumed combat. On August 26, in what became known as Second Manassas, Pratt was ordered to protect the battalion's right flank, under heavy attack from Stonewall Jackson's division. In less than 20 minutes, half the regiment was down, as were six color bearers.

According to Witkowski's account from Osborne, Pratt's horse was shot from under him, after which he led his troops against the enemy on foot, sword in hand. Advancing into a wood, Pratt was hit in the right shoulder by "buck and ball" (a 0.69-caliber bullet in one barrel, heavy buckshot in the other). The buckshot passed through the colonel's shoulder into his neck and to his spine. He was instantly paralyzed from the neck down, though he was still coherent. An officer attempting to carry him from the field was shot down. Others rallied around their colonel. Seward Osborne convinced the federal Park Service to erect a plaque where Pratt fell.

Pratt was removed to a hotel in

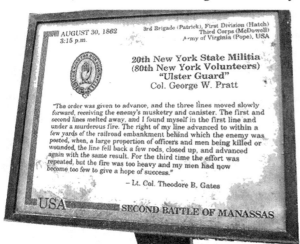

Plaque at Manassas, Virginia

Alexandria, Virginia, where he was attended for a few days by a body servant. Showing little improvement, he was taken by train to Albany on September 4. Governor Morgan visited him on September 9 and recommended to President Lincoln that Pratt be promoted to brevet (temporary battle rank) brigadier general. It never happened. The family gathered on September 11. After "smoking a good cigar," Pratt died.

His funeral on September 14 at St. Peter's Episcopal Church was said by the *New York Times* to be the largest Albany had ever seen. He was buried in Albany Rural Cemetery. Anna Pratt survived her husband by almost 60 years, his son by only five. In memory of the colonel, his father, who died in 1871, had a large stone (Pratt Rock) placed at the entrance of Prattsville depicting father and son.

The unit Pratt led, also known as the 80th NYS Volunteers (so dubbed when the 20th, organized as a militia, joined the Federal army), marched on. It fought at South Mountain, Antietam, Fredericksburg and Gettysburg, where it took heavy losses in repulsing Pickett's charge. A monument to the regiment stands at Gettysburg on McPherson Ridge to this day.

The original lecture was presented by historian Walter Witkowski on May 17, 2013.

11.

Samuel D. Coykendall: Kingston's Forgotten Tycoon

City Historian Ed Ford delivered a lecture on Kingston's wealthiest family, the nineteenth- and early twentieth-century Cornell-Coykendall clan. His talk was the eleventh edition of the "Kingston's Buried Treasures" series.

This time, the subjects were quite literally buried in front of the 70 attendees. The commemoration of the 100th anniversary of Samuel D. Coykendall's death was held at the family gravesite at Montrepose Cemetery. While organizers probably didn't intend it that way, the siting of the talk offered an object lesson in the concept "you can't take it with you."

"S.D.," as he was known in his lifetime (1837–1913), is buried with his father-in-law and their families on a hilltop. In death as well as in life, the family dominated its

Samuel Coykendall

surroundings. In fact, Cornell owned much of the land on which Montrepose Cemetery in midtown Kingston is located.

Lecture participants enjoyed balmy, bug-free weather with cool breezes as Ford delivered his one-hour lecture. It could have been worse.

The Iron Fist of Kingston's Industrial Boom

"Ed, being a stickler for detail, wanted to hold the event on January 14, the actual date of Coykendall's centennial, at the graves, but we talked him out of it," program moderator Paul O'Neill disclosed.

The Cornell-Coykendall family came to dominate local transportation by steamship, barge, rail and trolley. Thomas Cornell at his death in 1890 was worth $700 million (in today's dollars), and his son-in-law about half that when he died in 1913. All of it was tax-free, O'Neill noted.

The half-century decline and eventual extinction of this billion-dollar empire after the death of Coykendall is a familiar business story. "They say a prosperous firm goes from shirtsleeve to shirtsleeve in three generations," noted Ken Darmstadt of Darmstadt Overhead Doors, a lecture regular, Kingston businessman and a descendant of Ezra (Cornell University) Cornell. "The first generation creates and builds the business, the second runs and expands it, the third spends all the money."

Samuel Coykendall, a humble dry-goods clerk with a talent for organization, came to Kingston in 1859. He had the good fortune to marry Cornell's daughter Mary Augusta after returning from the Civil War in 1865. (Mary's Avenue and Augusta Street are named for her.) Cornell, then in the prime of an expanding business career, recognized the young man's talents, took him into his business, and in time made him a virtual partner. In addition to tugboats, steamships, railroads, trolley lines, hotels, and interests in ice, bluestone and cement, the two dealt extensively in real estate. In 1898, for instance, when the 108-mile D&H Canal ceased operation, Coykendall bought the right of way for $10,000 and sold its parcels for considerable profit.

O'Neill, who participated in the question-and-answer session following Ford's speech, said it is difficult to imagine today the scope of Cornell-Coykendall enterprises. "At one point, almost everyone in Kingston worked for Cornell or Coykendall, one way or the other," he said. "If you told some of those people at the turn of the twentieth century it would all be gone in 50 years, they would have been astonished."

Towing on the Hudson

The Cornell towing company on the Rondout, which repaired company tugs and locomotives, alone employed some 450 workers in the 1880s.

Ford, born only five years after Coykendall died, mused about the company's employee relations in an era notorious for worker abuse. "I have no idea how friendly they were or how good they were to people, but I hope they were," he said.

Cornell was known to have an open-door policy. "It didn't matter who you were," Ford said. "He'd always talk to you, though you might have to wait awhile."

Cornell and Coykendall "always seemed to be ahead of the curve," Ford said, "even with the rapid growth following the Civil War. They were visionaries."

Coykendall's six sons, all of whom either graduated from Columbia University with degrees in civil engineering or attended the school, were granted equal shares of his estate upon his death in 1913. Though Ford said the record wasn't entirely clear, it appears that sibling rivalry was a factor in the company's relatively swift decline. So was an inability to keep pace with innovations in the family's core transportation businesses. The Kingston *Daily Freeman* first announced in 1901, for instance, that plans were under way to convert the 60 Cornell tugs plying the Hudson at the time from coal to oil. With the

Children of S.D. Coykendall: (*Seated:* Frank, Catherine & Robert. *Back:* Frederick, Edward, Harry &Thomas)

Coykendall brothers at odds, however, that transition was not begun until 1924.

Samuel Coykendall, who lived in a mansion atop West Chestnut Street in Kingston, was perforce a major influence in Kingston. He was a trustee of Kingston Hospital at the turn of the twentieth century and influential in building the Carnegie Library across the street. He contributed generously to a project to relocate the remains of Governor George Clinton from Washington, D.C., where he was buried to the Old Dutch Churchyard in 1908.

Coykendall contributed several thousand dollars to the publication of an Old Dutch genealogy. The Coykendall science center at SUNY New Paltz is named for his son, Edward. Another son, Frederick, was chairman of the Columbia University board of directors that named Dwight Eisenhower as college president in 1948.

Augusta Coykendall was a noted clubwoman and philanthropist. Some of the Coykendall brothers never married. Others died young with no children. A sister had two. There are no

Coykendall Mansion on West Chestnut Street

Coykendalls living in the area, according to Ford. The dearth of heirs combined with the decline in business and high living dissipated the family fortune in relatively short order.

Their hilltop gravesite, testimony to power and prestige, has been in decline for years. Its once-shining white marble columns and headstones are now a dull gray. Restoration plans are underway, though probably without contributions from the estates of the dead moguls.

The original lecture was presented by Kingston City Historian Edwin Ford on June 21, 2013.

12.

The History of Kingston's Press Corps: The Rough & Tumble Story of Kingston's Newspapers

On a sweltering Friday evening, journalist Hugh Reynolds educated and entertained a capacity crowd at the twelfth installment of the "Kingston's Buried Treasures" lecture series, with "The History of Kingston's Press Corps, The Rough and Tumble Story of Kingston's Newspapers." Reynolds traced the history of local journalism from the *Ulster County Gazette*'s coverage of the death of George Washington to the most recent makeover of the *Daily Freeman*. He interspersed his 90-minute lecture at the Senate House Museum in Kingston with notes, quotes and anecdotes from his long career in local journalism. Reynolds worked for the *Daily Freeman* from 1966 to 1976 and again from 1984 to 2008. He was a co-founder of the *Ulster County Gazette* in 1976 and owned it until 1984. His column, "City Beat," ran in both papers as a regular feature. Reynolds, after having been let go by the *Freeman* in 2008 in a cost-cutting move, currently writes for Ulster Publishing, which publishes weekly newspapers in Woodstock, New Paltz, Saugerties and Kingston.

Ulster County had literally dozens

It Wasn't Always Pretty—The Daily Freeman and Beyond

of weekly newspapers before and after the *Rondout Daily Freeman* was founded in 1871. The newspaper's name, Reynolds suggested, may have been rooted in the antebellum abolitionist movement when a "freeman" was an emancipated slave. Several newspapers in the North, but none in the South, carried that name according to Reynolds. A *Rondout Weekly* preceded the daily by more than 25 years. Weeklies were published in larger towns around the county on a regular basis from the *Ellenville Journal* to the *Saugerties Post*. Weeklies tended to rise and fall with political movements, carrying names like *Republican, Democrat, Kingstonian, Argus* and *Chronicle*.

The *Freeman* underwent several name, ownership and location changes before being acquired by 27-year-old Jay Klock in 1891. Under Klock's astute management, the *Freeman* grew to become one of the leading dailies in the Mid-Hudson region. Klock died in 1936, leaving the newspaper to his widow, Lucia, who subsequently sold the paper to a newspaper chain in 1966. She established the Klock Foundation, which has dispensed millions of dollars to local charities, non-profits and hospitals in the decades since. The *Freeman*, which relocated its offices from Rondout to Hurley Avenue in 1974, became a morning paper in 1987 and has gone through several ownership changes in recent years.

Reynolds's anecdotes about the figures he has covered, from Nelson Rockefeller to Hamilton Fish, G. Gordon Liddy, Frank Koenig, Maurice Hinchey and Kevin Cahill, drew laughter and applause from the overflowing crowd. Reynolds's projections on the future of print newspapers in an increasingly paperless society were anything but optimistic. He speculated the *Daily Freeman* might contract to three days a week in the near future, but that other well-established weeklies might in turn expand their coverage. Local newspapers

Nelson Rockefeller, G. Gordon Liddy and Frank Koenig

will have to increase their emphasis on local news in order to remain viable, as did their predecessors, he said.

Reynolds also opined that the internet will continue to deliver news often based on innuendo, gossip and rumor. The ability to report behind the cloak of anonymity should be a grave concern, he warned. That diligent, responsible, professional journalism was everywhere under stress, primarily for financial reasons, was equally troubling.

In response to audience comments criticizing the *Freeman*'s most recent makeover as difficult to navigate and read, Reynolds reflected that readers tend to be resistant to change.

The original lecture was presented by journalist Hugh Reynolds on July 19, 2013.

13.

Kingston City Hall:
The House That United Kingston

The story of Kingston's City Hall at 420 Broadway, termed "Kingston's symbol" by Alderman Tom Hoffay at the thirteenth installment of the "Kingston's Buried Treasures" lecture series, closely parallels the city's modern history. Born of compromise and necessity, the building is located near the boundary of the former villages of Kingston and Rondout. In its almost 140-year history, the City Hall has endured devastating fire, long abandonment and urban flight. It has been twice saved and restored to former glory.

Kingston City Hall

The building's story, according to Hoffay, a midtown Democratic alderman who represents the historic uptown Stockade District, begins in the years immediately following the Civil War, when Kingston boasted three population centers. The village of Kingston on the Esopus Creek was the county government center, Republican and as an agricultural and banking center relatively wealthy. The hamlet of Wilbur on the Rondout, a smaller settlement, was a busy locus for bluestone traffic.

The area between the village lines in midtown Kingston was rocky, hilly and only sparsely populated, Hoffay

The Glue Between Kingston and Rondout

said. Broadway, called Union Avenue in those days, connected the two villages.

While distinctly different in terms of population and commerce—and fierce rivals—the two villages had transportation, banking and newspapers in common. Both were growing rapidly after the Civil War. Their leaders became convinced, however, that village government was unable to keep pace with development.

View from City Hall – early 20th Century

Rondout village on the Rondout Creek "was a sort of a Wild West," Hoffay said, a portal for immigrants where half the population spoke a native language other than English. One of the busier ports on the Hudson River, Rondout shipped coal via the D&H canal and bluestone and cement on the Hudson River. According to Hoffay, Rondout leaders first came up with the notion of creating a city around 1870—named Rondout, naturally.

The state assembly took some two years to debate the issue. Politically powerful Kingston, with Fair Street Assemblyman Dr. Robert Loughran, a veteran of the Ulster Guard in the Civil War, sponsoring the legislation, won the name game, much to the chagrin of Rondout. The *Rondout Daily Freeman*, which later changed its name to the *Daily Freeman* in recognition, apparently, of the merger, declared that "the hatchet is buried."

For a long time, the hatchet wasn't really buried. But the two villages found something in common, a City Hall located at a neutral site to reflect concrete compromise and a new era. One of the first acts of the city government elected in April 1872 was to name a committee to purchase land for a new City Hall. There were at the time nine wards with two aldermen each. The first mayor, James Lindsley, manager of a cement works in Ponckhockie, was a Republican from Rondout.

The property, about two wooded, rocky acres located on a 600-foot hill (above sea level) was purchased from John O'Reilly, an Irish immigrant who had prospered in real estate speculation. O'Reilly owned most of the land that is now considered Kingston's civic center. His mansion was located on the hill across Broadway where Kingston High School was built in 1915. The school's front wall on Broadway and entrance gates fronted the O'Reilly estate. O'Reilly Street is named for the family.

The original building, designed by architect Arthur Crooks, was in the high Victorian Gothic style popular at the time. Its tower is a replica of that on the Palazzo Vecchio in Florence, Italy. The common council authorized up to $60,000 in bonding for the building, with the state chipping in another $20,000. Built during 1873 and 1874, it opened in May 1875. During construction, the government met at the nearby Schwalbach's Hotel, later the Grand Central Hotel.

The new building contained about 16,000 square feet on four floors, including the attic. The mayor's and clerk's offices were on the first floor with the police department and city court. The common council occupied the second floor, and other government offices were on the third floor. A carpenter's shop in the attic was mostly used for storage. The building contained a two-cell jail with a separate entrance for defendants.

The building had wooden floors and staircases and extensive wooden paneling. Heat was supplied by fireplaces at the end of each floor. Built on solid rock, the brick-faced building had no basement.

A fire, which probably started in the carpenter's shop, broke out at twilight on June 4, 1927, and quickly consumed the tower. Witnesses, observing the holocaust from the lawn of Kingston High School, told of the bell in the bell tower crashing through the wooden floors, "clanging all the

City Hall afire - 1927

way down." Firefighters summoned from a firehouse a block away were unable to quench the blaze. The building was a total loss.

There was, however, no rush to reconstruction. A three-man committee of prominent city architects appointed by the council recommended a new building "more in the colonial style," Hoffay said. No dice. "This was the symbol of Kingston and it had to be restored," Hoffay said.

Instead, the council opted to rebuild a "fireproof" building onsite, effectively encasing "the bones" of the original. "Just about every piece of wood was replaced with concrete, steel or marble," Hoffay reported. "They never wanted that building to burn again, and ultimately that's what saved it."

The Vecchio tower was modernized, the front entrance lowered and redesigned, and the roof line and chimneys capped off. Operating systems were updated. The building reopened in 1929, at an estimated reconstruction cost of $200,000, with the common council moving into its ornate chambers on the third floor.

And yet, in only about 35 years, through depression, war and urban flight, the building fell into such a state of disrepair that some elements in Kingston were calling for a new City Hall. This was a plank in Raymond Garraghan's successful 1965 mayoral platform.

While the City Hall was declining—some said through deliberate neglect—Rondout urban renewal was wiping out some 50 acres of century-old buildings in Broadway East between St. Mary's Church on Broadway and the Rondout Creek. Garraghan was reelected by a historic (Democratic) majority in 1967 on a vow to build a new City Hall in Rondout. He reasoned, and most of the members of the common council agreed, that a new City Hall would promote redevelopment in Broadway East. Garraghan also argued it that would be foolhardy to invest money in a dysfunctional, deteriorating City Hall with no elevator and extremely limited parking.

Construction of the Rondout City Hall began under the Garraghan administration and was completed by his successor, Frank Koenig, elected in 1969. What then became known as "old City Hall" was abandoned by government in early 1972. "The city simply locked the doors and walked away," Hoffay told his audience at the City Hall last week. The windows were not boarded up; leaks in the roof were left to worsen. Pigeons nested where aldermen once wrestled, and abandoned records rotted in the attic.

"The only thing that saved the building from more than 20 years of neglect was its fireproof reconstruction," Hoffay said. "It was a disgrace to the city, but it was structurally sound."

Unsuccessful efforts by the Friends of Historic Kingston to prevent the abandonment of the building and then to stabilize it for future use were led by City Historian Ed Ford.

"Ed Ford carried the torch for a lot of years," Hoffay said, to applause from an audience of about 60 people, including Ford. At one point, the adjacent Kingston Hospital expressed interest in converting the building into medical facilities, but nothing came of it.

Freshman Assemblyman Maurice Hinchey secured a $500,000 state matching grant to restore City Hall in 1975, the total price tag for restoring the building and installing an elevator having been estimated at $1 million. With more than $1 million already spent on Rondout City Hall and government leaders in opposition, Kingstonians voted against the proposal at referendum that year. The grant went back to Albany.

In 1998, two-term mayor T.R. Gallo, having freed up some bond money after paying off sewer construction debt, convinced the common council (unanimously) to borrow $6.5 million for the restoration of City Hall. It was Gallo's late father, Alderman-at-Large T. Robert Gallo (1968–1977), who with Garraghan and Koenig had led the charge to build a new City Hall. "It was the right decision then and it's the right decision now," said Koenig, contacted shortly before the re-opening of the building in 2000.

Common Council Chamber

Over a 30-year span, those decisions, with some federal and state aid, cost city taxpayers about $10 million (in addition to interest on bonds). The sum included construction and conversion of the Rondout City Hall (over $2 million) and an estimated $7.3 million and counting at the old City Hall.

Still left uncompleted at what is again known as the City Hall is some $500,000 in roof repairs in the tower, which had leaked into the council chambers. Earlier, granite front steps installed in 2000 had to be replaced. Also to be finished are three $15,000 lunettes in the council chambers, one of which will be dedicated to City Historian Ed Ford. (The Ed Ford Lunette was dedicated in Kingston City Hall on September 6, 2014.)

Editor's note: Hugh Reynolds was the Freeman's City Hall reporter from 1967 to 1976 and covered most of the stories on the relocation and reconstruction of the City Hall during that period.

The original lecture was presented by Kingston Alderman Tom Hoffay on August 16, 2013.

Significant Dates in the History of the Kingston City Hall

March 29, 1872—The state assembly approves legislation to merge the villages of Rondout and Kingston into a new city called Kingston.

April 16, 1872—The first election in the new city calls for a mayor and nine wards with two aldermen in each.

May, 1873—The Common Council approves purchase of a hilltop lot on Broadway from the O'Reilly family. Construction starts on a new City Hall. Project cost is estimated at $100,000.

May 21, 1875—The first meeting of the Kingston Common Council in the new City Hall.

June 4, 1927—Fire erupts in the attic of City Hall. The building is gutted. Common council authorizes up to $200,000 for restoration.

May 7, 1929—Common council meets for the first time in the restored, modernized City Hall.

January–February 1972—City abandons Broadway City Hall for a new City Hall on Garraghan Drive in Rondout. Construction costs estimated at $1 million.

April 27, 1998—Common council authorizes $6.1 million in bonds to restore old City Hall.

May 21, 2000—Refurbished City Hall is formally dedicated. Construction costs exceed $7.3 million (with federal and state grants). Police department and city court remain at Garraghan Drive.

14.

Christoffel "Kit" Davits: Kingston's Original Rebel

Christoffel "Kit" Davits, one of early Kingston's most enigmatic characters, was probably a founding father of the colony, and certainly one of the first permanent settlers in Rondout. This "original rebel" preferred the company of Native Americans in the region with whom he traded, drank and, no doubt, brawled.

Davits was profiled by noted author and local historian Marc Fried at the fourteenth installment of "Kingston's Buried Treasures" at the Senate House Museum on September 20. About 65 persons attended.

Like Wiltwyck founder Thomas Chambers, an Englishman fluent in Dutch, Davits could speak many tongues. He

Trading with the natives

A Rascal Remembered

learned the various languages and dialects of Native Americans from Albany to Manhattan. His ability to communicate with the indigenous folk set him up as a trader in two illegal trades—selling alcohol and beaver pelts.

Born in England about 1615, Kit

Early map of New Netherlands

Davits (also known as Christopher) first attracted public attention after a brawl in a tavern in Dutch New Amsterdam around 1638, where he was accused of striking a servant and another man with a tankard. Several similar incidents were noted in the early court records.

Settling in Fort Orange (Albany), Davits plied his trade up and down the Hudson. At some point he must have encountered the fertile farmland around the Esopus Creek. Davits was among land speculators who visited the area in 1650 (including Chambers). Unlike the others, he did not purchase property. Fried suggested that Davits might have been more of a "middleman" because of his linguistic skills. Davits bought 12 acres of land on the Rondout Creek near the Strand in 1653 and settled there with his family.

Davits was charged with "selling brandy to the savages" later that year. His sales of liquor, which he brewed in Rondout, led to charges of "inciting the Indians against the Christian community." He pleaded not guilty.

Fried spoke of "a consistent pattern of fights, inciting Indians and poor administration of his wife's estate." Davits, Fried concluded, was "clearly viewed with suspicion, distrust and not liked." He was a rascal.

Some 360 years later, Fried, while admitting that much of his presentation was the product of "logical assumption, since documentation is sparing," has come to a more charitable conclusion. "My choice has always been to like him."

"He had a proclivity for mischief," Fried conceded. "His relationships with the Indians were opportunistic, but my former professor Harry Matzen [at SUNY and UCCC] once said that if he had had a choice of sitting down with Thomas Chambers or Kit Davits, there's no question whose company would be more fascinating."

At critical junctures, Davits's virtues outweighed his faults. His talents as an interpreter and his relationships with local Indians were invaluable to the fledgling European communities in the region. Davits served as an interpreter in the First Esopus War (1659) and was summoned from Fort Orange in 1663 for similar duties in the Second Esopus War. He accompanied a punitive mission of colonial troops to the Shawangunk and Vernooykill area to rescue 23 hostages taken by Indians at Kingston.

OLD^E VLSTER

Vol. X   APRIL, 1914   No. 4

Christopher, or "Kit" Davis, ♪ ♪ ♪ ♪ the Esopus Pioneer

The Esopus people were never a serious threat after the burning of their villages and crops and the killing of some 50 tribal members. Smallpox and other European diseases for which Native Americans had no immunity were the greatest killers, wiping out 90 percent of the indigenous population between 1600 and 1700, Fried told his audience.

Despite an adventurous life, Davits departed "with more of a whimper than a bang," Fried said. The exact date of his death and burial are unknown, but the last public mention of him was in 1677, Fried told his audience.

Fried, a resident of Wawarsing, is the author of five books on local history, beginning with *The Early History of Kingston and Ulster County* (1975), *Tales from the Shawangunk Mountains: A Naturalist's Musings; A Bushwhacker's Guide* (1981), *The Huckleberry Pickers: A Raucous History of the Shawangunk Mountains* (1995), *Shawangunk Mountains: A Mountain Wilderness* (1998), and *Shawangunk Places and Names* (2005).

The original lecture was presented by author and historian Marc Fried on September 20, 2013.

15.

Rondout: The Boom Years

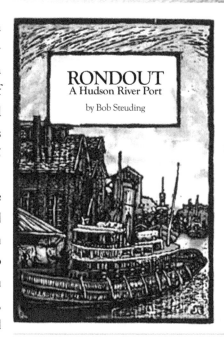

RONDOUT
A Hudson River Port
by Bob Steuding

The story of Rondout's rise from sleepy upriver agriculture shipping port in the early nineteenth century to its half-century of boom times as the nexus of the extraction and transport of coal, bluestone, ice and cement has been well documented in Bob Steuding's 1995 book, *Rondout, A Hudson River Port*.

Steuding, in an address before the fifteenth installment of "Kingston's Buried Treasures" series, offered much more than the thumbnail sketches of the characters who fueled Rondout's rise. It was an era when robber barons—locally, the likes of Wurts, Von Beck, Hone, Cornell, Coykendall and Tremper—made tax-free fortunes on the backs of cheap immigrant labor. Rondout owed its initial industrial prosperity to the D&H Canal, which connected the coal mines around Honesdale, Pennsylvania, to the Hudson River from 1828 to 1898. Rondout, according to Steuding, was a "dangerous" pestilent place where pigs ran wild in the unpaved, garbage-strewn

Rise and Fall—The Long Arc of Rondout's Past

streets, eating refuse and sometimes rooting out corpses from hillside cemeteries.

"It was a very dusty, noisy, polluted place," Steuding told his audience at the Senate House Museum in uptown Kingston. And crowded. Steuding estimated the habitable area in Rondout at about 200 acres. Jammed into that area along the creek and a few hundred yards upland were perhaps as many as 10,000 people.

Breweries and saloons abounded. People drank beer. It was safer than water. Plagues, probably cholera from polluted water, struck four times in the 1840s, culminating with over 400 deaths in the last big outbreak in 1849. "There were no hospitals and few doctors," Steuding said. Public health issues began to be addressed in the 1850s.

Labor was cheap and plentiful. Eight cents a day was the going rate. A brickmaker was supposed to produce at least 1,000 bricks a day, Steuding said.

Gangs roamed the streets, one of the more infamous being a bunch of "Americanists" called the Bumblebee Boys. They were soon badly outnumbered by Irish, Italian and German immigrants.

Rondout in those days was defined as a much broader area than in modern times. It included Ponckhockie (sometimes called North Rondout) to the east, Wilbur to the west, and upland areas like West Chestnut Street and President's Place, where the wealthy built their mansions to escape the stench, noise and pestilence of the riverfront.

Rondout was divided east and west by Broadway, originally called the Plank Road and later, Union Avenue. The west was "the canal side," with street names of canalmen and business leaders like Abeel, Wurts and Rogers. The east side, demolished by urban renewal in the 1960s, had names like Hasbrouck, Lindsley, Chambers and Cordts. The limestone industry was centered in the east, with caves that reached 100 feet into hillsides.

The careers of Thomas Cornell (1814–1890) and his son-in-law Samuel Decker Coykendall (1837–1913) roughly parallel the rise and decline of Rondout. Cornell, who arrived in Eddyville (Lock No. 1 of

Samuel
Coykendall

Thomas Cornell

the D&H) the year his future son-in-law was born, built a shipping and commercial empire. Coykendall and his sons expanded and managed it, selling off sections of the abandoned canal to adjacent property owners.

Kingston Point circa 1900

The Coykendall era featured the building of Kingston Point amusement park (with a Ferris wheel), docks for the river Dayliners, and trains connecting the Catskills to the Hudson. In 1903, Kingston Point had an estimated one million visitors.

To Steuding, the beginning of the end for Rondout coincided with its merger with Kingston in 1872, two years after the canal's peak year. The new city's first mayor was a riverfront limestone manufacturing manager but population and power gradually shifted uptown. In 1898, the D&H closed. "It was already over," Steuding said. "Rondout was obsolete," its manufacturing base gone, its shipping taken over by freight railroads.

In 1913 Coykendall died. In 1921, the Oriental Hotel at Kingston Point burned to the ground. In 1932, the Ulster and Delaware Railroad went bankrupt. In 1948, the last Dayliner docked at Kingston Point.

In 1961 the planning firm Raymond and May reported that 16 percent of Rondout was vacant. Its population had declined by half since its peak 90 years earlier. The average income of $1,250 a year in Rondout was half that of uptown. "It was the place where poor people lived," Steuding said.

The planners recommended massive demolition and redevelopment on the east side of Broadway and along the creekfront. Millions in federal grants were available.

City officials in the late 1960s authorized construction of a new City Hall in Rondout, which they hoped would attract development. In the early 1970s, the *Daily Freeman*, a Rondout fixture since 1871, considered building a new plant on urban renewal property, but instead relocated to Hurley Avenue. A new bridge over the Rondout at about that time further diverted traffic from Rondout.

Public housing was built in the late 1960s to accommodate some of the more than 3,000 people who had been evacuated by urban renewal. Private housing followed in the early 1980s. There are still acres of empty space in what was once called Broadway East. The "canal side" of Broadway was only lightly touched by urban renewal, its largest building being the abandoned Orpheum Theater at Spring Street. A neighborhood center was built on the site.

These days Rondout is a busy port of call for pleasure craft and the occasional river liner. Millions in federal funds over a decade have produced a creekfront renovation that attracts numerous visitors. Shops and restaurants do a brisk business in the summer and autumn months. Winters are slow.

"Old Rondout had slipped its moorings and disappeared in the mists of time," Steuding summed up. "But Rondout survived urban renewal, even at half what it once was."

This historian has a voice. He concluded by singing aloud a Willie Nelson–like song written in 1913 called "Dear Old Rondout."

The original lecture was presented by author and historian Bob Steuding on October 18, 2013.

16.

Arthur Flemming: Kingston's National Statesman

Arthur Flemming

To people of a certain age, the Flemmings (Flemings) they are likely to remember might be figure skater Peggy, Sir Alexander (inventor of penicillin), Ian (James Bond author), Victor (director) and/or original *Jeopardy* host Art Fleming. But there's another, closer to home: Arthur S. Flemming, cabinet secretary, advisor to presidents and college president.

Assemblyman Kevin Cahill spoke on the life and contributions of Flemming, a native Kingstonian and advisor to eight U.S. presidents, at the sixteenth installment of the "Kingston's Buried Treasures" lecture series at the Senate House Museum. "Arthur Flemming is not just a Kingston buried treasure, he's a national buried treasure," Cahill said. His subject is buried in the family plot in Montrepose Cemetery.

Cahill, as a young assemblyman, was a Flemming Scholar, even though he said that at the time "I didn't know who he was." Selected state legislators are given training in public policy and advocacy, based on the career of Flemming.

Former Health and Human Services secretary Donna Shalala said at the time of Flemming's death in

> *"One of the great intellects of (American) social policy."*

Virginia in 1996, he "was one of the great intellects of social policy, [who] combined an extraordinary knowledge with a rare gift for policymaking." Cahill said he met Flemming in 1994 or 1995 at a Kingston Hospital centennial celebration event.

Cahill presented a study of a complex character, a native son "who never forgot his roots," a cabinet officer and advisor to presidents for over 40 years, president of three colleges, and two-time recipient (from Dwight Eisenhower and Bill Clinton) of the Medal of Freedom, the nation's highest civilian honor.

Cahill, who spoke before about 75 attendees at the museum, described Flemming (1905–1996) as "a man who whispered into the ears of people who whispered to the president." He had, in a word, influence.

Born on West Chestnut Street in Kingston to a bank president and Ulster County Surrogates Court Judge and a homemaker, Flemming distinguished himself in the Kingston High School Class of 1922 as a debater. On weekends he preached at local churches.

Laura Bailey (later Terpening and sister to J. Watson Bailey) was an influential teacher who instilled in Flemming a desire for public service. She convinced him to attend her alma mater, liberal progressive Ohio Wesleyan College. Flemming would later become president of that college. But before going to college, Flemming took a year off to work as a reporter for the *Daily Freeman*. As a teenager, the precocious Flemming wrote the newspaper's editorial endorsement of Calvin Coolidge in 1924, according to Cahill.

Flemming moved to Washington, D.C., shortly after graduating from Wesleyan in 1927. He pursued graduate degrees and worked at the newspaper that would become *U.S. News and World Report*. While in school he met his future wife Bernice, a native of West Virginia and a Democrat. Flemming and his wife had four children; none live in the area. Flemming earned a law degree from George Washington University, though he never practiced.

His first influential position was as one of three civil service commissioners appointed by President Franklin Roosevelt in 1938, a post he held until 1948. Flemming established civil service examinations for various positions and encouraged the hiring of women and African-Americans. With war imminent, he was assigned to a team to convert the economy to a war footing. At the end of the war, President Harry Truman appointed him to the Hoover Commission on organizing the executive branch of government.

"Flemming had an incredibly close relationship with former President [Herbert] Hoover," Cahill said. Hoover, then the only living ex-president, spoke at Flemming's investiture as Wesleyan president in 1949. Flemming was later president of Oregon State University. President Truman named Flemming to the Atomic Energy Commission, which advised the president on atomic energy policy.

President Eisenhower asked Flemming to return to Washington as the third Secretary of the Health, Education and Welfare Department, but Flemming, immersed in his duties as college president, at first declined. "He asked his father for advice," Cahill said. "He called his family every Sunday. His father told him it was his duty to accept the presidential assignment."

"You just don't say no to the President of the United States," Cahill said the elder Flemming advised his son.

Flemming was known for (quietly) enforcing anti-segregation laws through the use (or withholding) of federal funding. He supported investment in higher education, cracked down on the fake colleges which were rampant at the time, and called attention to issues of air, water and land pollution, Cahill said. "And this was before Rachel Carson's *Silent Spring*," he added.

Flemming was an early supporter of fluoridation, a movement fiercely resisted in his home town. Having been an advocate of health care for the elderly and Social Security since the Roosevelt administration, he chaired the first White House Conference on Aging under Eisenhower. What was known as "The Flemming Plan" died in Congress in 1960, but re-emerged as Medicare under the Johnson administration five years later.

Flemming is perhaps best known for what was called "The Great Cranberry Scare" of 1959. Given evidence that cranberry growers were using an extremely toxic substance as a pesticide, Flemming called for a halt to all sales of cranberries two weeks before Thanksgiving. The uproar was seismic, but led to stricter oversight of pesticides in the nation's food supply.

Flemming clashed with Barry Goldwater over the future presidential nominee's insistence on removing liberal planks from the Republican platform in 1960. "Given the closeness of that presidential race [against John F. Kennedy], we can only wonder if inclusion of those planks might have made a difference," Cahill said. Flemming backed Lyndon Johnson against Goldwater in 1964. He was a drafter of the Medicare Act of 1965 and an advisor to Nixon on expansion of Medicare in 1972.

Flemming was fired from the U.S. Civil Rights Commission by Ronald Reagan, the last president he served. "He accepted it but didn't like being fired by press release," Cahill said.

His name lives on in the annual Arthur S. Flemming Award for excellence in government.

The original lecture was presented by New York State Assemblyman Kevin Cahill on November 15, 2013.

17.

Kingston's Bluestone Industry: The Rock That Paved a Nation

The Ulster County bluestone industry at its peak in the mid-to-late nineteenth century employed upwards of 10,000 men. So said Dr. Peter Roberts Jr. in his presentation at the Senate House Museum in Kingston on the local bluestone industry, "The Rock That Paved a Nation." Roberts's talk was the seventeenth in the "Kingston's Buried Treasures" series of lectures on local history and historical figures.

Bluestone waiting to be shipped

Bluestone, a form of sandstone, was buried for eons, mined for decades, and often transported by teams of eight horses and a wagon for shipment from ports from Malden to Wilbur to the nation's major metropolitan areas, principally New York City.

Bluestone has the quality of being attractive, durable and workable. "And it's not slippery when wet," Roberts told his audience of about 60 persons. These virtues were modestly proclaimed by the president of Friends of Historic Kingston without the slightest sign of undue favoritism. Bluestone of a less superior quality is still mined in Delaware County, he said.

A Hard Look at America's Walkways

Bluestone was mined in quarries throughout Saugerties, Woodstock, West Hurley and Marbletown, from pits involving as few as a family to hundreds of miners. Support industries included teamsters and boatmen.

Mining of bluestone would be considered an environmental disaster these days, which is one reason it's no longer mined here, Roberts said. Sometimes, he said, bluestone was buried beneath 20 feet of cover and earth. Since miners were only interested in marketable slabs, more than half the stone mined was left in the quarry as slag. Heaps of nineteenth-century slag top 30 feet in some areas of Ulster County. Water has filled in many of the old quarries.

A Bluestone Quarry

The stone is found in distinct horizontal layers, which were extracted with wedges, sledgehammers and iron bars for leverage. "It was amazing how much stone a few men could mine," Roberts said, showing slides of rough-looking, sturdy nineteenth-century quarrymen posing at their mines.

Stoneworkers were for the most part immigrant Irish, Roberts said, known for hard work and hard drinking. They settled near mines in Quarryville, Jockey Hill in the town of Kingston and beneath Overlook Mountain in Woodstock (California Quarry). Some of the largest mines, covered over by the Ashokan Reservoir in West Hurley, were abandoned by the time the reservoir was built in the early twentieth century.

Large bluestone slab being transported on Wall Street

Transporting stone to port, a trip of between ten and 15 miles over rough roads, accounted for an estimated 20 percent of the cost of producing the product, Robert said.

The bluestone era began in the 1830s, peaked in the 1870s and was just about over by the turn of the century, according to Roberts's research.

For the miners, "It was pretty messy work," Roberts said, what with noise, dust and the backbreaking chore of loading tons of bluestone on wagons or onto barges. Blacksmiths served the vital function of fashioning and sharpening tools and making the iron rings for wagon wheels.

Bluestone forest

Monument to Bluestone – Opus 40

Harvey Fite's Opus 40 in Mount Marion, built between 1938 and 1976 when Fite died in an accident at the site, is the sculptor's testament to the bluestone industry. One of the largest sites that can still be visited is the bluestone forest at Lake Onteora off Route 28, said to be the size of three football fields.

Bluestone is used primarily for sidewalks, but also for foundations. Only occasionally, due to its high cost, is it used for building construction. The most prominent bluestone structure in the county is the Old Dutch Church (1852) in Kingston's Stockade district. St. Francis de Sales Church in Phoenicia and the Morton Memorial Library in Pine Hill, both built in 1902, and the Zen Monastery in Mount Tremper are other examples of bluestone construction.

"The perfect bluestone slab"

Nineteenth-century millionaires, including Kingston's own Thomas Cornell, were willing to pay large sums for "the perfect bluestone slab" to showcase their homes, Roberts said. William Vanderbilt ordered a 20-foot by 15-foot slab for his Fifth Avenue mansion sidewalk in 1881, at a cost of $10,000, or about $225,000 in today's dollars.

Such slabs were rarely shipped, however. "For that, you had to have a buyer," Roberts said. Most such slabs were cut up for sidewalks at shoreline processing plants.

At one time the Fitch Company of Wilbur was the largest bluestone dealer in the nation. Fitch House, built in 1870 and still standing next to the Rondout Creek, was constructed entirely of bluestone.

The arrival of rail lines to the Rondout in the 1870s enhanced the bluestone business for a while. In short order, however, less expensive Portland cement replaced bluestone and local limestone cement as the sidewalk materials of choice. By the 1890s, the bluestone era was almost over.

Roberts credited Lowell Thing, a former president of the Friends of Historic Kingston, "for starting me on this great bluestone adventure." Thing's home on West Chestnut Street features one of Kingston's more prominent bluestone entrances.

The original lecture was presented by Friends of Historic Kingston President Dr. Peter Roberts on December 14, 2013.

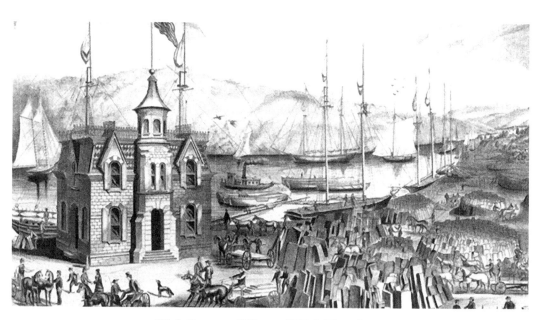

Fitch House – Offices of Fitch Bluestone

18.

The D&H Canal: Kingston's Corridor to Prosperity

The names of a few streets in Downtown Kingston named after its founders like Wurts, Jervis, and McEntee, plus a few viaducts, locks, embankments and indentations in the ground in various municipalities, are all that remains of the Delaware & Hudson Canal. That and some earth-filled ditches south and west of Rondout. But for 70 years ending in 1898, the D&H was the transportation lifeline that put Ulster County and its home port on the Rondout Creek on the map.

The hand-dug canal transversed 108 miles of rugged wilderness on an almost direct path northeast from the coal fields of Honesdale, Pennsylvania, to Port Jervis and from there northward to the sleepy port of Rondout in Kingston. The self-contained ditch, originally 32 feet wide at the top, 20 feet at the bottom and four feet deep, could accommodate up to 30-ton barges hauled by mules along adjacent tow paths. At its peak in the 1850s, the

Putting Rondout on the Map

widened canal could carry boats more than four times larger in both directions.

In Ulster County the canal paralleled Route 209 (the Mine Road) and the Rondout Creek. Like the Erie Canal, the D&H revolutionized local overland transportation, reducing freight costs and travel time by up to 90 percent. Towns and villages sprang up along its route where only the occasional farm had existed. For half a century, the D&H Canal made Rondout the busiest port on the Hudson River.

"Its impact on the future of Kingston cannot be measured," Bill Merchant, president of the High Falls–based Delaware & Hudson Canal Society, told an overflow audience at the eighteenth monthly installment of the "Kingston's Buried

Barges on the D&H Canal

Treasures" lecture series at the Senate House Museum. Merchant, who regularly conducts tours of the five locks near his home in High Falls, presented 86 slides of the canal, some dating to the 1850s.

The canal was the vision of the Wurts brothers, Maurice and William, who owned anthracite coal fields around Carbondale, Pennsylvania. They later shipped to what would become Honesdale, named for another canal executive/investor and a future mayor of New York City. With the Philadelphia market glutted by readily available nearby coal, the brothers sought an overland route to ship anthracite coal from

Maurice and William Wurts

Workers digging the Canal

mines to port to New York City.

There were no assurances that early nineteenth-century New York would continue as the nation's largest city. But the brothers raised $1.5 million from investors, and with some government subsidies, work on the canal began in 1825. Employing mostly Irish and German immigrant labor and the expertise of engineers who had learned their trade from working on the Erie Canal, construction began on the D&H on almost the same day as the Erie Canal opened in 1828. John Roebling, whose son built the Brooklyn Bridge (with Rosendale cement), was the design engineer. The D&H, said to be the first privately funded million-dollar enterprise in America, began to pay dividends to investors within five years of operation.

The canal was similar to a tenant-farmer operation where the owners maintained the system to operate its 108 locks, while boatmen leasing their craft from the company paid a fee to haul product. Typically, it took about five years to pay off the cost of the boat.

It was grueling, demanding work. "I don't think I've ever worked that hard a day in my life like those men did every day," Merchant told his audience.

The shipping season ran from about mid-April to early November, when the canals typically froze over. Boatmen often worked in the winter in the ice harvesting or bluestone businesses. The discovery of

John Roebling

cement in High Falls during the canal digging led to the Rosendale cement industry, another large employer of off-season boatmen.

While coal transport exceeded a million tons a year at its peak, the canal also carried

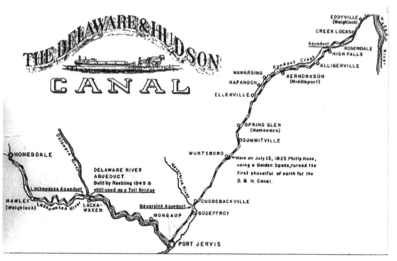

Route of the D&H Canal

all manner of local produce and industry to market. Merchant noted that many of the towns along the canal had larger populations in the mid-nineteenth century than they do now.

While it kept to its original route, the canal evolved during its operation. A deeper, wider trench allowed larger boats to travel in both directions. Ninety-foot boats could be barged directly to New York City on the Hudson River, eliminating the need to offload barges onto boats at Island Dock in Rondout. The canal company purchased and used one of the first locomotives in America.

Merchant, an antiques dealer in Kingston and New Paltz, said he was aware of a few songs written about the D&H Canal, but not as many as those about the more celebrated Erie.

The widespread construction of railroads following the Civil War brought the canals' rapid decline. Railroads could transport goods cheaper year-round. The last load of coal shipped by the D&H left Honesdale in November 1898.

Kingston industrialist Sam Coykendall then purchased the canal route from High Falls to Kingston to ship Rosendale cement. Purchased for something less than a nickel on the dollar (compared to the original cost of the canal), Coykendall's operations lasted for about a decade. Empty canal boats lined the Rondout in Kingston for years afterward. Merchant said the Army Corps of Engineers burned the boats in the early 1950s.

The history of the D&H Canal is preserved and interpreted by the D&H Canal Society.

The original lecture was presented by D&H Canal Museum President William Merchant on January 18, 2014.

19

The McEntees:
Kingston's First Family

Other than a pair of street names and some still-life and landscape paintings among private collections, there's little left of Kingston's nineteenth-century McEntees, in their time one of the city's more prominent families.

During the 1800s, the family would produce a D&H Canal engineer, a Civil War Army officer who played a key role in the battle of Gettysburg and two prominent artists, one of whom befriended the brother of a presidential assassin.

The McEntees

Civil War Photos: Seward Osborn Collection

Commerce and land speculation were among the family's other enterprises.

The McEntee family (pronounced Mack-en-tee) was chronicled by Kingston historian Lowell Thing at the nineteenth edition of "Kingston's Buried Treasures" at the Senate House Museum.

Kingston's Royals

Thing, who lives at 55 West Chestnut Street on property once owned by the McEntee family, has written a book called *The Street That Built a City: McEntee's Chestnut Street, Kingston, and the Rise of New*

York [published in 2016]. Thing's home was built in 1898 by Henry Crispell, son of Dr. Abraham Crispell, one of the first residents on the street.

Charles McEntee, the Scotch-Irish son of Northern Ireland Protestants, emigrated to this country in the late eighteenth century, settling near Utica. James McEntee, the first noteworthy member of the family, was born on a farm near Herkimer in 1800. He died in 1886. James, through some family connections, worked on a survey crew on the Erie Canal near Utica in 1819. "He learned on the job," said Thing, at a time when West Point was the only school in the nation to offer engineering courses. After five years on the Erie Canal, he rose to assistant engineer. James McEntee came to Kingston in 1825 as an engineer on the Delaware & Hudson Canal, then under construction.

The family lived in what is now the Senate House in Uptown Kingston, but tragedy struck in 1826 when James's wife and child died in childbirth. He married Sarah Tremper of Kingston in 1829. Their first child, Jervis, the future painter, was born in 1831 in what is now known as the Mansion House at the foot of Broadway.

McEntee was involved in building the first Rondout lighthouse in 1837, the Eddyville dam in 1839 and Island Dock in 1845. He also acquired boats for towing on the Hudson. That phase of his career ended when one of the boats he captained sank off Yonkers.

James McEntee

Once the D&H Canal was completed in 1828, James McEntee, according to Thing, entered various businesses, including coal mining in Pennsylvania at the terminus of the canal, a dry goods store in Rondout and real estate speculation in and around Rondout.

He was apparently a man of vision, purchasing some 52 acres of land overlooking Rondout, part of which encompasses the West Chestnut Historic District with its sweeping views east and west. Thing said McEntee, an experienced surveyor by that point in his life, laid out most of the building lots on West Chestnut, which he then sold to prosperous merchants and canal executives. McEntee built the first home on West Chestnut in 1851.

Jervis McEntee, named for a D&H canal engineer, was something of a self-taught child

The McEntee home painted by Jervis McEntee - 1881

prodigy. At 19 he was showing his landscapes at the National Academy in New York and the following year began studying with Frederic Church. The two Hudson River School artists were lifelong friends. McEntee died in 1891.

Landscape architect Calvert Vaux married McEntee's daughter Mary in 1854. He's buried in the McEntee family section in Montrepose Cemetery.

Julia McEntee Dillon (1834–1919) was a classically trained artist educated in Paris and known for her still-life painting. Illustrated books on both McEntee artists are available at the Johnston Museum on Main Street in Kingston.

By the age of 27, Jervis McEntee was making his living as an artist in New York City, though he frequently painted at his studio in Kingston.

Landscape by Jervis McEntee - 1880

(Left) **"Still Life" by Julia McEntee Dillon**

Three McEntee brothers served in the Civil War, Jervis, John and Maurice. Their cousin, Captain John McEntee, served under Colonel George Sharpe, head of military intelligence for the Union Army. Sharpe and McEntee, his officer in the field, are given credit for tracking Robert E. Lee's Army of Northern Virginia as it marched through Maryland

Photo: Seward Osborn Collection

Maurice McEntee

and into Pennsylvania, thus giving the Federals vital intelligence. "Without that intelligence, the battle of Gettysburg might have turned out very differently, and with it, American history," Thing told his audience.

Jervis McEntee and his wife were friends with the actor Edwin Booth, brother of John Wilkes Booth, during the Civil War. Thing said the McEntees were instrumental in helping Edwin Booth register and vote for Abraham Lincoln in 1864. After Lincoln's death they vouched for Edwin Booth as loyal to the Union.

The McEntee homestead and studio, located at the south end of what is now Dietz Court near the former site of the Coykendall mansion, was torn down shortly after the death of Sarah McEntee in 1903, its last family occupant. The mansion was demolished in the early 1950s.

There are remnants of the McEntee artist studio at 99 West Chestnut Street, a home built by Gerard McEntee, near its junction with Orchard Place. Recent renovation revealed family artifacts, said Thing.

The original lecture was presented by author and historian Lowell Thing on February 15, 2014. (Photos by permission of author unless otherwise indicated)

20.

Kingston at the Battle of Gettysburg: The Ulster 20th and 120th

I t was the shortest event in the long-running "Kingston's Buried Treasures" series at the Senate House Museum, but the most graphic. To many in the audience, it was one of the best.

Gary Schussler of Zena, an avid Civil War enthusiast, recounted the history of two of Ulster's own regiments, the 20th Ulster Guard and the 120th. The latter, raised by Colonel George Sharpe, fought in decisive engagements of the three-day battle July 1–3, 1863 at Gettysburg.

Schussler assembled a Ken Burns–like documentary which included still photos, battlefield scenes, maps showing deployment of the two Ulster regiments, music by Molly Mason and Jay Unger (also featured in the highly acclaimed Burns series on the war), and voiceovers by local people.

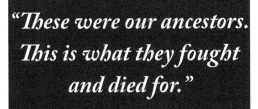

"These were our ancestors. This is what they fought and died for."

"I wasn't sure it was going to work when Gary played a few snippets for me," conceded Paul O'Neill, series host and the voice of George Sharpe. The loud applause from a large audience that night left no doubt he had succeeded.

"I thought it was excellent," said Kingston American Legion Commander Bill Bittner, with his wife, Kathy, a regular at the lecture series. "My eyes were wide open all the time. I wasn't yawning." Bittner, a gun enthusiast, owns an original 1858 Springfield muzzle load rifle of the kind used in the Civil War.

Bittner, like many families in the area, has a direct connection to the battle of Gettysburg. "My ancestor, Christopher Bittner, was known in the family as a bit of a rogue," he explained. "He left [Kingston] when the war broke out, for some unspecified legal reasons, but wound up enlisting with a Pennsylvania outfit. He was killed on Seminary Ridge the third day of the battle. I've seen his name on the Pennsylvania monument that was erected there."

There are three monuments to the Ulster men who fought in the battle. One commemorated the 20th delaying a Confederate advance west of Gettysburg in early fighting on the first day of the battle. A second stands in the peach orchard where the 120th engaged in heavy combat on the second day. The third, in honor of the Ulster Guard, was erected on Cemetery Ridge where Pickett's desperate charge was repulsed on the last day of the decisive battle.

Of interest, Schussler said, was that Sharpe, who raised the 120th Ulster and Greene county volunteers in 1862, did not personally lead his men onto the field at Gettysburg. Colonel Cornelius (C.D.) Westbrook was in command.

Sharpe had been assigned to the Army of the Potomac headquarters as chief of its military intelligence operations months prior to the battle. Many historians credit Sharpe's pinpointing movements of the Confederate Army as it marched north toward Harrisburg, Pennsylvania, its objective, for giving Union forces a decisive advantage at Gettysburg. Sharpe continued supplying intelligence during the battle.

Sharpe, who died in 1900, erected a monument to his men on the battlefield after the war, and another on the grounds of Kingston's Old Dutch Church, where he was an elder.

Civil War historian Seward Osborne of Olivebridge dedicated a monument to the 20th on July 3, 1981. Schussler said Sharpe's monument to his men, erected in 1896 in the Old Dutch Church cemetery, inspired him to further research local connections to the Civil War. Schussler, who retired last year, worked in the county office building across the street.

"Seward is the source," Schussler said of the self-taught Civil War scholar many consider the preeminent local authority on the Ulster Guard.

Schussler had passed the monument many times, he said, "but one day I took a good look and it struck me that these were our ancestors, this is what they fought and died for." Both sides suffered catastrophic casualties at Gettysburg in close-quarter fighting, fierce charges against heavily defended objectives, and heavy cannonades. About 150,000 soldiers fought in the three-day battle, and about 45,000, about evenly divided on both sides, were killed, wounded, taken prisoner, or missing in action.

The Ulster regiments suffered some of the heaviest casualties. According to Schussler, the Ulster Guard entered the battle with 375 men, of whom 35 were killed, 111 were wounded (some of whom died later), and 24 were missing, an attrition rate of 45 percent. The 120th mustered 427 men, of whom 33 were killed, 154 wounded and 17 missing— almost half the unit.

Casualty figures show how the Civil War ground down men through disease (by an estimated two-to-one ratio to combat deaths), battle and desertion. The Ulster Guard left Kingston in October of 1861 with around 800 men, the 120th with 900. Some 21 months later, going into Gettysburg, those two regiments had lost almost half their strength.

Some wounded members of the Ulster Guard went into "veterans reserve" after Gettysburg, but the regiment saw considerable action in the 22 months remaining in the war. So did the 120th. Sharpe, by then a major general, was in the room when Robert E. Lee signed surrender

Monument to the 120th – Gettysburg

Battle of Gettysburg

documents at Appomattox Court House, Virginia, on April 9, 1865.

The Senate House Museum's continuing presentation of Civil War artifacts in its extensive collection is offered on Sundays from 1 to 4 p.m. at the Loughran House next to the Museum on Fair Street. There is no charge.

The original lecture was presented by Civil War historian Gary Schussler on March 15, 2014.

21.

The Old Dutch: The Church That Sculpted Kingston

R ather than taking his listeners down the familiar historical paths of people, dates and places, Rob Sweeney chose to discuss the impact of religion and culture on history. It was a topic fitting for an elder of Kingston's Old Dutch Church and a direct descendant on his maternal side of its seventeenth-century founders.

But while Sweeney spoke extensively to a history of triumph over adversity and tragedy and of religious freedom, he also touched on some darker sides of prejudice and exclusion. He spoke of the reform of religious institutions over time.

Kingston's Old Dutch Church, the "mother church" of dozens of other Reformed congregations in the area, was

Old Dutch Church

> *"It was a melting pot, but you were expected to become like them."*

once one of its most exclusive. A church that then and now considers its members among God's chosen has become in recent years one of the area's more inclusive congregations.

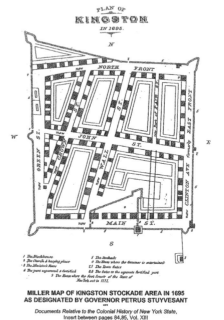

MILLER MAP OF KINGSTON STOCKADE AREA IN 1695
AS DESIGNATED BY GOVERNOR PETRUS STUYVESANT

Documents Relative to the Colonial History of New York State,
Insert between pages 84,85, Vol. XIII

Sweeney's 75-minute lecture, the twenty-first in the "Kingston's Buried Treasures" series, delved into the history of the sixteenth- and seventeenth-century Reformation movements in the Netherlands and Germany. It traced the Dutch Reformed Church from its origins in wars against Catholic Spain and other sects to New Netherlands and finally to Kingston (Wiltwyck) in the 1650s.

The Dutch West India Company settled New Netherlands on the tip of Manhattan about a dozen years after Henry Hudson's exploration of what was then known as the North River. It seems that the settlement was not as inclusive as popular legend would suggest, Sweeney told his audience at the Senate House Museum. "They were not going to have Catholics or Quakers causing problems in the New World," Sweeney said. The colony offered freedom of conscience, but Catholics were not free to worship publicly.

"It was a melting pot, but you were expected to become like them," he said. The governing group tolerated Presbyterians and Congregationalists as having fundamentally similar Calvinist beliefs. Quakers and Lutherans were suppressed. There was only one state religion, and elected officials were required to be members of that church. Others had no right of free assembly, though all were required to pay taxes to the church.

Director Peter Stuyvesant, the son of a Calvinist minister, initially banned the immigration of Jews to the new colony until his orders were "strongly" countermanded by Dutch West India officers in Amsterdam. "The Dutch [whose religion was steeped in the

Old Testament] believed Jews were essential to the second coming of Christ," Sweeney said. "Jewish merchants were also heavily invested in the Dutch West India Company."

Unlike the Founding Fathers of the American Revolution, the Dutch rulers firmly believed in the combination of church and state. Religion, they believed, played an active role in public affairs. Much like the Israelites, the Dutch saw themselves, Sweeney said, as God's chosen people. The early Dutch, he said, were ruled by commerce and religion, what has come down as the Protestant work ethic. "It was the culture in which the church was formed," he said. "Remember, people live in a culture. A church isn't just a building. It's theology."

Nowhere is the contrast among structure, theology and practice more dramatically demonstrated than in the two church buildings that now face each other across Main Street, the (1852) Old Dutch Church and St. Joseph's (1868) Catholic Church.

Ten years after the establishment of the First Reformed Protestant Dutch Church of Kingston in 1659, the first church building, a two-room wooden structure, was raised near the site of the present church. A stone church that replaced it was burned by the

Old Dutch Church

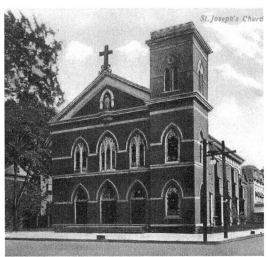

St. Joseph's Church

British in 1777, but rebuilt in time to host a visit by George Washington in 1782. The congregation built a brick church (now St. Joseph's) across the street in the 1830s.

The present structure, a national historic landmark, was built in 1852. The congregation sold its former building (now St. Joseph's) to the state, which established an armory there. It was stipulated in the sale that the building could not be sold to Catholics for a church. The state put the building on the market after the Civil War.

Old Dutch legend has it that Luke Noone, a wealthy Kingston Catholic, bought the building from the state and donated it to the church. A new state armory was built on Broadway in 1878.

The early Dutch church served multiple purposes as a community center, including from time to time as a village hall and courtroom, a schoolhouse, a home to the church *domine* (Dutch for minister), and when necessary as a debtor prison. St. Joseph's was used almost exclusively as a house of worship.

Sweeney showed slides contrasting the interiors of St. Joseph's during its Old Dutch period and in its Catholic renovation. What Sweeney described as "an architectural treasure" is little changed since its completion more than 160 years ago. The Tiffany stained-glass window in the nave of the church was installed in 1893 in memory of the Houghtaling family.

Sweeney said he had many other tales to tell of the Old Dutch, whose records are extensive and well-preserved. Since time constraints for "Kingston's Buried Treasures" lectures were limiting, he asked to be invited back.

The original lecture was presented by Old Dutch Church Elder Rob Sweeney on April 19, 2014.

22.

A Place to Call Home:
A Century of Immigration

First in trickles, then in droves, the Dutch (obviously), Germans and Irish first, then the Italians, Poles, African-Americans and many others, came to Kingston. Different people from different places with different cultures and religions settled in ethnic enclaves with their own churches, schools and businesses. Bitterly resisted by "Know Nothing" nativists here for centuries previous, by sheer force of numbers and dint of will, immigrants to Kingston came to dominate the city, its politics, commerce and education.

Former Kingston City Alderman Tom Hoffay talked about a century of immigration (roughly between 1825 and 1920) in the twenty-second edition of the "Kingston's Buried Treasures" lecture series at the Senate House in Kingston.

In 1820, the last census before the initial wave of immigrants, what later became the City of Kingston had a population of about 3,000, about equally divided between the villages of

"By 1900, immigrants had transformed Kingston."

Lower Broadway – Rondout

Kingston and Rondout. Over the next 40 years, that population increased to about 16,000, about two-thirds of it in Rondout.

"There were ships and trains arriving every day from the port of New York," Hoffay said. Railroads constructed after the Civil War carried immigrants to the interior and points west, north and south.

As Hoffay described it, life in 1820 in Kingston's rebuilt Stockade was "settled, secure and predictable." There was one church, the Old Dutch on Main Street. "You knew everybody and probably were related to everybody," said Hoffay. "The governor had lived here. The village (the county seat) had enormous political power."

Then came the immigrants. The first wave worked on the construction of the D&H Canal, which opened for a 70-year run in 1828. Others became engaged in constructing Rondout's tenement-style buildings to house the flood of immigrants and their growing families. Bars and brothels abounded. The first Catholic Church in Kingston, St. Mary's on Broadway, opened in 1835. St. Joseph's in uptown Kingston was founded in 1868.

The second wave of immigrants was driven by political unrest, if not revolution, on the European Continent and by the Irish famine in the 1840s. A Celtic cross, erected by the Hibernian Society a few years ago on the lawn of St. Mary's, commemorates "the Great Hunger," listing the names of local Irish families who settled here. The German immigration also included Jews from Germany, Russia and Poland, fleeing to America for religious freedom like the earliest Dutch settlers of Kingston. The city's first synagogue, Temple Emanuel, traces its history to the Rondout of that era.

The formation of German and Italian states in the latter part of the nineteenth century led to another wave of immigration, as did unrest in the Polish provinces. Hoffay

St. Mary's Church

told his audience that wars, which often unite people of different backgrounds in common cause, were great levelers. Young immigrant males, many with military experience from the European conflicts of the 1840s, rose to leadership positions during the Civil War. Those who survived came home to assume similar positions in the community.

"By 1900, immigrants had transformed Kingston," Hoffay said.

Temple Emanuel

The Life of O'Reilly

Central Broadway landowner and businessman John O'Reilly was one immigrant who prospered in post–Civil War Kingston. O'Reilly, who immigrated in 1860, at one time owned the land where now stands Kingston City Hall, Kingston High School, the Carnegie Library, Kingston Hospital and the American Legion, "the very core of the city," Hoffay said.

At the time, the census recorded 19 houses of worship in Kingston and Rondout. The African-American population peaked at about 10 percent in 1820 (including Sojourner Truth) when slavery was still legal in New York State. While there was an influx of Southern immigrants after World War II, many local African-American families can trace their roots to the Civil War or even the Colonial era.

The anti-immigrant nativist movement in the 1850s, as represented by the Know Nothing Party, was active in Kingston, at one time holding a majority on the village board. Bias lingered in the forms of tension, hatred and vilification, Hoffay said. But a transformation took place after the American entry in World War I in 1917, Hoffay said.

"You see it on the plaque erected in front of City Hall just after the war," Hoffay said, displaying a photo of the celebration. "It's still there. Read the names. Those are the sons and daughters of immigrants."

While marriage between nationalities was unusual in the early years, these days Kingston is a melting pot from many places. A recent wave of Hispanic immigrants has added a different element to the city collage.

Organizations founded during the immigrant era, such as the Polish White Eagle Society, St. Mary's Benevolent Society, Germania Hall and the Knights of Columbus, endure but are generally in decline, something Hoffay finds unfortunate, given the rich heritage they represent. Of late, a rejuvenated Irish-Hibernian Society has been busy creating a cultural center on Abeel Street, high on a hill overlooking the Rondout Creek where the ancestors of many of its members arrived here many generations ago. The recently restored Reher Bakery on lower Broadway, envisioned as a cultural center for Jewish and other immigrants' history, gives visitors a view of life downtown in the nineteenth and early twentieth centuries. Another group is recruiting membership in a newly formed Italian-American society.

The original lecture was presented by former Kingston Alderman Tom Hoffay on May 16, 2014.

23.

The Early Stockade and Its Settlers: Pioneers of a Nation

Accurate descriptions of Kingston's original Stockade, built between 1658 and 1677, have eluded historians for centuries. And no wonder. The definitive 1695 original "Miller map" of the area went to the bottom of the Atlantic Ocean after its creator's ship was attacked by French privateers. The Rev. John Miller, who survived capture, later re-created the map from memory.

Local history buff and author Ted Dietz told this whale of a tale at the twenty-third episode of the "Kingston's Buried Treasures" series at the Senate House on Fair Street in Kingston.

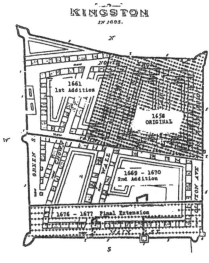

The Stockade

Dietz detailed Miller's appointment in 1692 as chaplain to British forces in "New York Territory." One of the Anglican minister's duties was mapping the several forts the British had established along the Hudson and Mohawk rivers after taking possession of the former Dutch colony in 1664. One of those forts was located in Kingston, said Dietz, "with six guns lined up on [what would become] Main Street."

When There Was a Wall

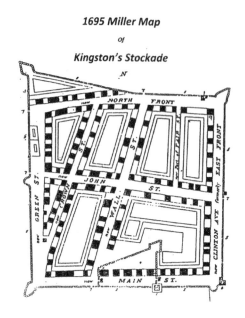

1695 Miller Map

of

Kingston's Stockade

Miller, who held a doctorate in theology from Edinburgh University in Scotland, walked the streets and byways of the Kingston Stockade and consulted recorded deeds in order to produce an accurate map. He also took notes on local animals, fish and fauna, with the intention of writing a book about New York.

Having completed his work, Miller sailed from New York Harbor in 1695. As his records contained "ticklish information about guns and such," Miller, for security reasons, threw everything overboard when the French attacked. After being released, Miller journeyed to London, where he reconstructed his records and maps from memory. Those records, filed in the Bishop of London's archives, remained undiscovered in the British Museum until 1843.

"So, for a period of almost 150 years, nobody saw a map of the Stockade," Dietz told his audience. He did not indicate whether anybody else had made maps of the area during that time. A London publisher issued the first book containing the map in 1862. Schoonmaker's 1888 history of Kingston makes extensive use of the Miller map.

Dietz said he doubted whether anyone could accurately recall exact details on an area of several hundred acres with more than 50 parcels. "We know mistakes were made," he said. "Miller had Wall Street connecting to North Front Street from John Street, and deeds on file clearly show that didn't happen before 1830. In fact, the deed filed by the father of John Vanderlyn [the artist] in the 1770s shows that house in the middle of Wall Street at John Street.

The fact is, it's the only map we have from that era, and it's believed to be largely accurate. Some things we just don't know," he said. Dietz said there was no description on the size of the lots—only their owners—on the Miller document. Streets remained officially unnamed into the early eighteenth century.

One indisputable service Miller provided for future generations was to accurately record lot owners (from deeds filed in the Stockade courthouse at the time and available to the public in the Ulster County Clerk's office on Fair Street). Names like Hendrick (the smith), Jan Schoonmaker (the carpenter), Jansen, Andries (the weaver), Barentsen, Casther the Norman, and two men named Stuyvesant speak to a working-class settlement.

A perusal of the lot owners connects some dots in Kingston history. "Lot No. 1," deeded to Wiltwyck founder Thomas Chambers, was located nearest to the nearby Esopus Creek. Chambers operated a brewery on his property and needed close proximity to fresh water. He hired Native American labor to work his farm along the creek, Dietz said, and paid in spirits. Indian drunkenness, as recorded elsewhere, may have been a factor in hostilities between settlers and natives.

Peter Stuyvesant

The Stockade, ordered and laid out by Dutch Governor Peter Stuyvesant in 1658 following an Indian uprising, was extended three times. The original Stockade enclosed North Front Street, John and Wall streets. In 1661 the west boundary was extended to Green Street (where the Hoffman House restaurant stands). The 1669–1670 extension moved the south boundary 300 feet south from John Street. The final extension in 1677 moved the south wall to Main Street, site of the orginal Old Dutch Church.

Dietz, who is 91, became ill toward the end of the scheduled hour-long lecture and was unable to finish. Lecture moderator Paul O'Neill wrapped up before calling emergency services to examine the speaker. Dietz was able to return to his nearby home unattended. "It could have been a case of lector anxiety," an EMT joked afterwards. Dietz later blamed a passing incident of vertigo.

"Ted is a terrific historian, very dedicated to his work," said a relieved O'Neill. "We are fortunate to have such people in our community who take an active interest in our history." Dietz is a retired New York City policeman who moved to Kingston in 1969.

The original lecture was presented by author and historian Ted Dietz on June 20, 2014.

24.

Our Buried Past: The Archeological Treasures of Kingston

From Abeel Street to Fair and points in between, Kingston's thousands of years of history lie just below the surface. It's the mission of Joseph Diamond, SUNY New Paltz anthropology professor, to dig it up, sort it out and try to figure out what it all means.

Diamond, presented as the region's "most prominent anthropologist" by program host Paul O'Neill, gave listeners at the twenty-fourth edition of the "Kingston's Buried Treasures" series sketches of digs done at the seventeenth-century Persen House at Crown

and John streets some 15 years ago, and along a stretch of Abeel from Ravine to Broadway last summer.

The artifacts Diamond and his teams found at those sites do not differ markedly from other digs in Kingston or on Huguenot Street in New Paltz. What struck some members of the audience at the Senate House in Kingston was how quickly Native American civilizations, some thousands of years in existence, disappeared after European settlement began in the early seventeenth century.

The Treasures Beneath Our Feet

There are numerous artifacts of these original peoples—projectile points, shards of pottery, beads and the like—but most of the stuff dug up, preserved and cataloged is from the comparatively recent European era.

Diamond, who takes students into the field every year, had most of the heavy lifting at the Abeel Street and Persen sites done by government. The city excavated Abeel Street to a depth last year in replacing water and sewer lines, leaving a temporary foot-wide trench along one side for Diamond and his crew to explore. They came up with 585 artifacts, he said, dating from pre-history about 8,000 years ago to the Dutch colonial era forward. More recent remnants, "Night Train and Mogen David" (wine bottles from the 1950s) were not cataloged, the anthropologist said, tongue obviously in cheek.

Diamond devoted much of his presentation to the Persen House, which was substantially restored by the county around the year 2000. Preservation architects took the interior down to the surface, exposing for Diamond and his crew an area that had not seen the light of day in centuries. They also studied the area around the county-owned building, now vacant, but open to tourists.

For Diamond, the date of demarcation was June 1663, the burning of the Persen House by marauding Indians. Beneath the "burn line," clearly visible in photographs presented during the lecture, is what amounts to ancient history. Above it, modern.

Of some note was that there is virtually no evidence of the second burning of the building by British forces in October

Artifacts from the Persen House

1777. Diamond had no explanation but some speculate that the building may not have been badly damaged or that it was quickly rebuilt.

Among the artifacts found were three cannonballs from the seventeenth century, perhaps gathered for the defense of the Stockade, glassware, stoneware, wine bottles with

their owners' personal seals, musket balls, flints, lice combs and remnants of a tailor shop. An early Persen was a tailor, one of the numerous businesses that operated at the site. A surgeon also practiced there.

Other artifacts offered evidence of the diets of early settlers: sturgeon, deer, elk and shark. "Why shark, we don't know," Diamond said. Also discovered was a handmade toothbrush made from a cow's rib.

Diamond's digs, which date back decades, "have considerably enhanced our understanding of our history," O'Neill said. There was also interior evidence from pole settings that the original (1658) Stockade ended at the Persen property.

Diamond said the building produced virtually no evidence of slaves, kept by whites until the 1820s. "Their slaves lived with the Dutch [and English], possibly in the basement where they cooked. It's hard to separate the whites from the blacks," Diamond said. They were certainly separate in death, as Diamond catalogued in a landmark 1990 study of the long-abandoned Pine Street African-American cemetery in midtown Kingston.

The original Persen House—it was built in four phases—probably had a thatch roof, like most of the buildings in the Stockade, but due to fire hazard, a tile roof after about 1700. Tiles were manufactured locally on a site near the present-day Deising's Bakery, Diamond said.

The original Stockade could not have been a pleasant place, as Diamond described it, with pigs and other animals running through the dirt streets and residents throwing garbage and the contents of chamber pots out into the narrow passageways. Artifacts uncovered centuries later speak to that colonial lifestyle, less so about the Native Americans all but extinct only a few generations after European settlement, or the African-Americans held in bondage there.

The original lecture was presented by professor and archeologist Joseph Diamond on July 18, 2014.

25.

From Dutch to English:
The Conquest of Kingston

Slaves in the early Dutch colonial era (circa 1625–1664) were treated rather better than those under English captivity, according to Ulster County Historian Anne Gordon. Though quite restricted, they were allowed to marry, congregate, attend religious services with whites, and in some cases were able to buy their freedom and own property. There were instances of intermarriage.

Women under Dutch rule were treated almost as co-equals of men. They could inherit and own property and businesses. "There were many women in business in New Amsterdam," Gordon said. Marriage was viewed as a partnership between equals.

That all changed when a fleet of English sailed into New Amsterdam Harbor 350 years ago and took possession of the Dutch colony. Hardly a shot was fired, Gordon told an audience of about 60 persons at the twenty-fifth edition of the "Kingston's Buried Treasures" series at the Senate House Museum.

Gordon said she had asked the

The Dying Days of the Dutch Dynasty

New Amsterdam – 1664

state to recognize the anniversary of the English takeover of New York—August 18, 1664—what she called "one of the most important events in our history," to no avail. "It has been shamefully neglected," she said.

But not by Gordon, whom lecture host Paul O'Neill called "a one-woman speaking tour."

While local militia manned the ramparts at the Battery, Dutch merchants quickly realized they had no chance against heavily armed English dragoons, possibly with reinforcement from the English colonies on Long Island and Connecticut. According to Gordon, the invading fleet comprised four warships and about 100 soldiers landing in Manhattan. Another 300 troops were disembarked at Brooklyn.

The Dutch petitioned their governor, the irascible and bellicose Peter Stuyvesant, to negotiate a surrender. Reluctantly, he did.

Dutch inhabitants were allowed to keep their property if they swore allegiance to the British Crown. The colony was renamed New York after the king's brother James, Duke of York, later King James II. James, who held vast estates in Ireland, was heavily involved in the slave trade.

Changes in status

For African-American slaves, English rule represented a transition to a different life of subjugation. The English afforded their slaves, considered "free labor," none of the limited privileges permitted by the Dutch. In 1712, slaves comprised 15 percent of the population of New York, Gordon said. That was a higher proportion at that time than in any Southern state.

Women also fared much worse under English common law. "The change in the status of women was dramatic," Gordon said. "A married couple was one person, and that was the husband."

Colonial affairs were strongly influenced by wars in Europe between countries seeking dominance in the New World. The Dutch briefly took back New York in 1673, but the English returned for good the following year. In 1683 the ten original counties, including Ulster, Dutchess, Orange and Albany, were established.

While Gordon described the English takeover as "bloodless," it was not without conflict. In Kingston, an English company of 70 men occupied the town and were lodged with local families. Disputes between the townsfolk, many of whom spoke no English, and the occupiers broke out. Relative peace was restored when 30 of the soldiers were granted 30 acres of land each in Marbletown in 1666, the year Wiltwyck and Nieuw Dorp were renamed Kingston and Hurley.

Ulster County remained a hotbed of unrest against foreign control, Gordon said. The pre–Revolutionary War slogan of "no taxation without representation" originated in Kingston, she told the audience.

The original lecture was presented by Ulster County Historian Anne Gordon on August 15, 2014.

26

Christopher Tappen:
Kingston's Unsung Hero

Ulster County Clerk Christopher Tappen is revered for saving public records from British invaders, a heroic deed performed 237 years ago.

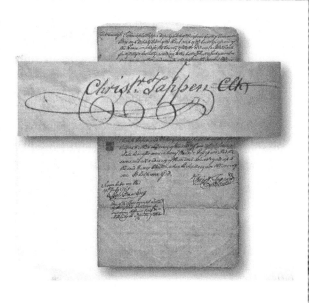

Given Tappen's 56-year tenure in the clerk's office, his signature is on more records than perhaps any other person in local history. He also served as delegate to three Provincial Congresses and in the state Senate and the Assembly. He was a founder of Kingston Academy and an original state Regent. Yet very little else is known about him. There is no known likeness of the man, despite his being a contemporary of John Vanderlyn of Kingston, one of the early republic's more prominent portrait artists.

The Man Who Saved Our History

"We don't know what he looked like and we're not even sure where he's buried. Probably in the Old Dutch Cemetery [at Wall and Main streets in uptown Kingston]," said current Clerk Nina Postupack, who spoke on the life of Tappen, "the man who saved history," at the twenty-fourth edition of the "Kingston Buried Treasures" series at the Senate House Museum. Postupack is the forty-fifth Ulster County clerk, heir to a line of succession dating to 1671 and the first woman to hold the office.

Tappen (1742–1826) was deputy clerk to George Clinton, his brother-in-law and by most accounts close friend and confidant, from 1765 to 1812. Clinton, whom Tappen referred to as "my brother," died as Vice President of the United States in Washington in 1812. Tappen served as the thirteenth county clerk until 1821, when he retired for health reasons.

For all practical purposes, Tappen was the county clerk even though Clinton held the

Gov. George Clinton

title from 1759 to 1812. Given his numerous important duties as general, state governor and two-term vice president, Clinton was seldom in Kingston, home of his wife, Cornelia Tappen, Christopher's sister. The Tappens lived in what was called "the executive mansion" (for Governor Clinton) on the corner of Wall and North Front streets. That stone house was demolished in 1868. The other "Tappen house" at Green and John streets was the home and office of Cornelius Tappen, a lawyer and son of Christopher. It is now an upscale restaurant.

"It might be possible that Clinton didn't know where the clerk's office was," program host Paul O'Neill quipped to laughs from an audience of about 65 people. The day-to-day duties and responsibilities of the clerk's office were left to Tappen. When war came to Kingston's narrow streets in mid-October 1777, Deputy Clerk Tappen was up to the task.

The popular saga of his saving Kingston's records from burning by British invaders in a hasty gathering of documents and a dash to the town of Rochester as redcoats marched up Broadway is partially true. The record suggests remarkable prescience on the part of Tappen and the governing Council of Safety, who upon learning of a large British force moving by barge up the Hudson on October 10 toward the state capital, ordered the town (which the mother country referred to as "that nest of rebels") evacuated and all official

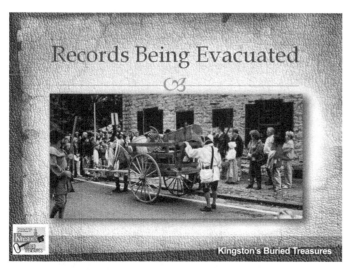

Biennial re-enactment of the Burning of Kingston

records moved. Over a three-day period, Tappen and others loaded documents into barrels to be placed in ten wagons for transport to Accord. British forces burned almost every building in Kingston three days later.

In 1778, the records were moved back to Marbletown, where Ulster County documents were separated from the state records shipped to the new capital at Poughkeepsie. Ulster records were returned to Kingston.

Those records, Postupack told her audience, were extensive, dating to before the Stockade Bond document in 1658. The records, from the mid-1650s to around 1710, are held in the county's collection at the Hall of Records on Foxhall Avenue. They were translated into English at the turn of the twentieth century.

Since the Dutch were in control of Kingston for only about a dozen years, with the British forces taking New Netherland over in 1664, the county's treasure trove of historical records is for the most part British and American. Those records, many in their original form, contain all manner of information, from tax records and assessments, to the proceedings of county government, court records, deeds, maps, mortgage recordings, marriage and military records.

"What is important about these records is that they tell stories," Postupack told her audience. "Because of these records we know how people lived during the early years of Kingston's history both under the Dutch and the English. Christopher Tappen was a link in this chain of record keepers."

Those records are maintained in a specially designed archival vault at the Hall of Records. Temperature and humidity are kept constant, and no one touches a record without permission and a set of white gloves.

Postupack, first elected clerk in 2005 after serving as chief deputy for more than 20 years, has made records accessibility, outreach and public education the hallmark of her tenure. "People ask me if they are the clerk's records, and I tell them they are not my records, or the county's. They belong to all the people and they are accessible to everyone," she said.

O'Neill declared Postupack as important a clerk as Tappen. "Christopher Tappen saved the records, but Nina has preserved them, secured them and made them available to all of us," he said. The records are also available online.

Former legislature chairman Richard Mathews, a regular attendee at "Buried Treasures" lectures, offered some perspective after Postupack's presentation. "Not to take anything from Nina and the clerk's office, but it was the legislature [at the urging of Postupack and former clerk Albert Spada 20 years ago] that appropriated the funding to establish the records center," he said.

And what of Christopher Tappen's remains?

Postupack said Old Dutch Church records list Tappen among its burials, probably on the site of the current church, built in 1852. Remains of those buried there were left in place, thus accounting for the relatively shallow foundation and subsequent structural issues suffered by the church building. Markers with an "X" (indicating bodies were under the church) were placed in the surrounding cemetery. There is no marker for Tappen, however. O'Neill and Postupack, who have worked closely in attempting to verify the location of Tappen's body, believe that at the least a marker should be placed in the cemetery for him.

Prior to the meeting's adjournment, Kingston photographer laureate Phyllis McCabe presented City Historian Edwin Ford with a commemorative book of her photographs of the dedication of a lunette in the historian's honor at City Hall two weeks ago.

The original lecture was presented by Ulster County Clerk Nina Postupack on September 19, 2014.

27.

The Burning of Kingston: The Phoenix Rises

The burning of Kingston by the British 237 years ago is a story oft told, foundational facts surrounded by legend. Less mentioned is the swift resurgence of the state's first capital from "utter devastation," in the words of First Ulster Militia re-enactor Hank Yost. The resurgence was testimony to a patriot spirit that simply would not allow the invaders to impose their will on the future of Kingston.

"If you stood on the bluff looking over what is now Hannaford's shortly after the British left, you would have had nothing behind you [essentially the Stockade area after 1695] but utter devastation. What had been a thriving metropolis was now gone, all gone," Yost told his audience at the twenty-seventh edition of the "Kingston's Buried Treasures" series. His lecture, "The Burning of Kingston: The Phoenix Rises," was given at the Senate House Museum before about 75 attendees.

You Can't Keep a Good Villain Down

"The houses were destroyed, people scattered, animals run off, smoke and stench hung in the air," Yost said. "It was truly a bleak, bleak time. With winter coming on, people were dependent on friends and relatives for shelter, or on good-hearted strangers."

Yet within days Kingston had begun its renaissance. With Captain Johannes Snyder, commander of the First Ulster Militia, and his troops pitching in, Kingstonians began rebuilding their town almost literally from the inside out. Some 300 buildings were torched by the British during the few hours they were in Kingston that autumn after- noon. Most, Yost said, were of the colonial

British warship in re-enactment

Dutch stone variety and were still standing. Gutted interiors were refurbished. Within a few weeks, residents of what had been "a thriving metropolis" of about 4,000 people began returning.

So rapid was Kingston's resurgence that the state's first capital, the place where the state constitution was drafted and its first government was seated in early 1777, was designated the capital three times over the next six years. Kingston, according to research provided by program host Paul O'Neill, was the state's capital from August to October of 1779, from April to July the following year and finally from January to March in 1783. George Washington paid a visit to the town in November 1782, about a year after hostilities ceased.

Yost, a retired police officer, has been a Revolutionary War re-enactor since the na- tion's bicentennial in 1976. He has participated in several re-enactments of the burning of Kingston and is a frequent lecturer on colonial military history.

Kingston, according to Yost, was the incidental vic- tim of a failed British military strategy for dividing the colonies. The goal, he said, had been to separate New England, the cradle of the revolution, from New York and the mid-Atlantic states and then conquer the colonies separately.

The original plan had British forces converging on Albany from the west along the Mohawk River, south from Montreal and north from New York City, which the British occupied in 1776. But British forces were defeated at the battles of Oriskany in the Mohawk

Valley and at Saratoga. British General Henry Clinton chose to attack Philadelphia in the autumn of 1777, rather than link up with General John Burgoyne's troops coming from the north. Instead the British sent a force under General John Vaughan upriver to assist Burgoyne in early October. Vaughan's "1,200 effectives," armed with rifles, 60 rounds of ammunition each, and bayonets, anchored off Esopus the night of October 15.

It is not clear when Vaughan learned of Burgoyne's surrender at Saratoga. Yost said Vaughan was informed by a spy as his force marched up what is now Delaware Avenue near Hasbrouck on the 16th after disembarking at Kingston Point. "He was hopping mad and he had three choices," Yost said. "He could continue upriver [toward Burgoyne], turn around and head south, or burn Kingston." Vaughan chose to attack what he called "that nest of villains."

Burgoyne surrendered on the 17th, the day after Vaughan burned Kingston. The spy's reference to British defeat may have been to an American victory at the Battle of Bemis Heights on October 7, one of the actions of the Saratoga campaign.

By the time Vaughan's force reached what is now Academy Green, the town had been evacuated, its animals scattered and its last few refugees were fleeing, heading north from near what is now Deising's Uptown Bakery. After leaving Kingston in ruins, Vaughan's force marched back to the Rondout, re-embarked on ships, and headed north against stiff winds, anchoring off Saugerties, from where it burned houses on the east shore of the Hudson.

George Clinton, commissioned a general in the Continental Army at the beginning of the war, was defending forts in southern Orange County when the British sailed upriver. That Kingston was left virtually undefended by Clinton has been a subject of some controversy. His entreaties to General Gates at Saratoga and General Putnam in Dutchess County (with a force of 6,000 men) for troops to protect Kingston went unheeded.

Legend has it that Clinton's advance relief force got to Snake Hill in Port Ewen (modern site of a radio transmission tower), where it could see smoke rising over Kingston to the west. By then, Vaughan had departed.

The biennial celebration of the burning of Kingston will take place next in October 2018.

The original lecture was presented by Revolutionary War Historian Hank Yost on October 17, 2014.

28.

The Senate House: Cradle of Democracy

SENATE HOUSE

1676

The state-operated 1676 Senate House in Kingston, the oldest public building in the United States, is one of the county's premier tourist attractions, drawing an estimated 20,000 visitors a year. Its archives contain national treasures like the John Vanderlyn (1775–1852) gallery, the largest collection of the artist's work.

But the Senate House, as its name implies, is best known for the few weeks in September 1777 when between 13 and 17 state senators met at the Clinton Avenue residence of a prominent Kingstonian. Members of the Assembly conferred at the Bogardus Tavern on Fair Street a few blocks away. Weeks later, the British raided the new state capital, burning down almost every building.

The Senate House with its wooden roof, floors and mostly wood construction was heavily damaged. Exterior rebuilding was in fieldstone and brick for the most part.

Home to a State, a Nation and Our Series

The property was acquired by the state in 1887.

Senate House Site Manager Thomas Kernan and Interpretive Programs Assistant Deana Preston spoke on its history at the twenty-eighth edition of "Kingston's Buried Treasures" at the Senate House Museum last week.

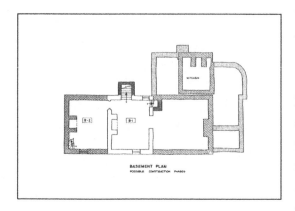

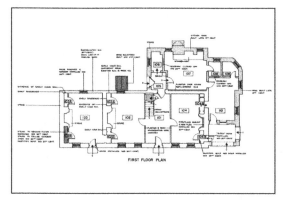

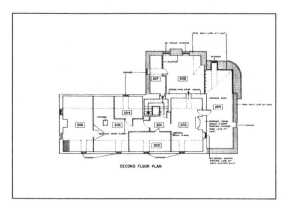

Senate House

Program chairman Paul O'Neill hailed the special relationship between the Senate House and the long-running lecture series. "We couldn't be closer to home, here in the Senate House," O'Neill said. "They open their doors to us every month [the site is closed to the public six months a year]. This is the cradle of our series." And by many accounts one of the cradles of the American Revolution.

Built in 1676 at the northeast corner of the Kingston Stockade by Wessel Ten Broeck, Preston said, the original brick building (its modern center) with wooden trim was about 20 by 25 feet with a kitchen in the basement. There were four additions, which included a store, a meeting room and a detached kitchen. Gables were added to expand second-floor bedrooms.

Preston traced the house's lineage from the Ten Broeck family to Abraham Van Gaasbeek, who owned the property during the Revolutionary War. It was Van Gaasbeek, wealthy sloop captain and trader, justice of the peace, trustee of Kingston Academy, militia officer and ardent patriot, who rented his meeting room to the State Senate. Contrary to some accounts, senators were not lodged at the Senate House.

Van Gaasbeek died in 1794, in his will leaving two slaves and his house to a niece. She married Peter Van Gaasbeek, Abraham's son and her first cousin, who died in 1797. Rented for a period of years, the house once served as a girls' school around 1827.

Sarah, daughter of Peter and Sarah Van Gaasbeek, died in the 1840s, leaving the house to a relative, Charles Westbrook. Westbrook was believed to have been the first person to call it the "oldest public house in America."

Preston said historian Marius Schoonmaker, husband of Elizabeth Van Gaasbeek, sold it to the state in 1887 for $8,000. Schoonmaker called it the Senate House in his history of Kingston.

Kernan said the philosophy of historic restorations in those days was to restore a property to what was perceived to be its original condition, what he called "faking the old." As a result, side porches were removed at the north and south ends of the house, but at the same time additions and separate entrances were added for staff. "It was changed externally to a significant extent," Kernan said. Internal work included heavy sanding of floors that had been installed after the British burning, repainting, and new windows.

Kernan said Supreme Court Judge Alfonso Clearwater, a Senate House trustee from 1887 to 1933, gave himself credit for convincing the state to purchase and renovate the property. Kernan offered an anecdote about the conflicts between Kingston and the state in managing the property during that period. In 1916, he said the city refused to extend gas lighting to the grounds of a state property, contending it was the state's responsibility. The state passed the buck back to the city.

Given conditions, "the morning harvest," as Kernan put it, could include "forgotten lingerie, whiskey and beer bottles." "We're amply lighted now and we still get some of the same harvest," he said to laughs from about 50 attendees. The three-acre grounds are open to the public from dawn until dusk.

The first major addition to the property occurred in 1927, the sesquicentennial of the burning of Kingston, with the dedication of the $100,000 Senate House Museum. The estate of Alton Parker, a former judge and 1904 Democratic presidential candidate, donated $10,000. Governor Al Smith laid the cornerstone. The building was completed in mid-1930. Its second floor was extensively renovated in the 1970s to create additional gallery space.

John Vanderlyn

O'Neill spoke about some of the historical figures associated with the Senate House. John Vanderlyn, then a struggling artist, was introduced to his most prominent patron, Aaron Burr, by Peter Van Gaasbeek, he said.

Kernan said most of the restoration work was done on the Senate House during the 1960s and 1970s. A copper roof was removed in 1977, amid much controversy, and replaced with original-looking wood shingles.

The nearby Loughran House on Fair Street, once the home of Civil War surgeon Dr. Robert Loughran, was sold to the Connor Funeral Home in 1924. The state purchased the property in 1968. It is used for staff offices, temporary exhibitions and special events.

The property, which contains two parking lots, also includes the early nineteenth-century Federal-style Abraham Masten House across Clinton Avenue, now used as an uptown Kingston visitor center.

The Senate House site is owned and operated by the New York State Parks and Recreation Department with headquarters at the Palisades Interstate Park Commission at Bear Mountain.

The original lecture was presented by Senate House Site Manager Tom Kernan and Interpretive Programs Assistant Deana Preston on November 21, 2014.

29.

Educating Kingston: The Spark That Ignited a Future

Kingston High School kicked off its 100th anniversary celebration in September 2015 by replicating a ceremony from 1914: students, faculty and staff, led by the KHS Tiger Marching Band, parading up Broadway to the venerable school edifice.

If not for two votes of the school board in the early 1970s, they might have been marching in a different direction—all the way to Lake Katrine. The plan at that time, which did not include reuse of the sprawling 27-acre Broadway campus, was to build a new high school on school-owned property near what is now Miller Middle School to replace a rapidly declining almost 60-year-old building. The plan was thwarted by a citizen group called WHITA (We've Had It Taxpayers Association), which elected an anti–new-building majority to the school board.

In the ensuing years, many millions of dollars have been spent on upgrading and renovating the Broadway facility. In 2013, voters approved a $137 million bond issue for major reconstruction of the Broadway campus. The state is

KHS
KINGSTON HIGH SCHOOL
100TH
ANNIVERSARY
1915-2015

A Century of Learning

expected to pay about 60 percent of the estimated construction costs.

Retired educator Anna Brett, who served at the school for 24 years of her 35-year career, rising from health teacher in 1973 to assistant principal in 1988 (she was appointed principal of Chambers Elementary School in 1997), spoke about the school and its history at the recent twenty-ninth "Kingston's Buried Treasures" lecture at the Senate House Museum.

Series host Paul O'Neill introduced Brett as someone who continues to serve the community through numerous organizations. She is a trustee of SUNY Ulster, where she did graduate work, and president of the Junior League of Kingston.

Prior to the construction of Kingston High School on Broadway in what had been known as "O'Reilly's woods," secondary students were served by three separate facilities: Kingston Academy on what is now Academy Green, Ulster Academy on West Chestnut Street (later one of Kingston's elementary schools) and Ponckhockie Free Academy in north Rondout. Brett spoke about the apprehension on how archrivals from Uptown and Downtown Kingston would mix at the central Broadway facility, strategically located across from the City Hall.

"Nothing happened," she noted.

The school, with architecture modeled after the Louvre in Paris, opened with the march on Broadway of about 800 students from grades 10 through 12, and 29 faculty. Freshmen were added in 1921. Included were students from what would decades later become the Onteora and Rondout Valley school districts.

The manual training "vocational" building (later named the Whiston Building) was added in 1929, and a

Kingston High School

swimming pool 50 years later. The site underwent major reconstruction with the addition of the Salzmann building in 1980. "It was a very difficult time to teach," Brett recalled. Plans for the latest reconstruction call for major work during summers through the 2016–2019 school years.

Published reports a century ago spoke of amazement at the size of the original building—its huge auditorium, cafeteria (lunch cost a quarter, about $5.75 in today's money) and student lockers. Boys and girls were taught in separate classes.

First Graduating class of KHS 1916

The day started with a sing-along in assembly, with Fred Van Etten at the piano. Charles Moulton (1915–1917) was the school's first principal. Dan Allen (1960–1983) served the longest tenure as principal, followed by Clarence Dumm (1932–1950), pronounced "doom." "You did not call him Mr. Dumb," Brett recounted to an elderly audience, some of whom recalled "the voice of doom."

The names of district educators—Meagher, Miller, Michael, Bailey, Myer, Walton, Finn, Cioni, Salzmann—grace the foyers of school district buildings.

KHS opened with 10 clubs and organizations. It now has over 60. The school newspaper, *Dame Rumor*, was launched in 1932 under the direction of English teacher Agnes Scott Smith, "Smitty" to her colleagues. The name was changed to *Highlights* in 1979. The "Fighting Maroon" became the Kingston Tigers around that time, though retaining school colors of maroon and gold. The May Queen and her court have been regular events since the beginning.

Myron J. Michael

Kate Walton was another original faculty member, a legendary math teacher and a strict disciplinarian. "Tough but fair," Brett said. The Kate Walton Field House, built in 1950, was named in her honor. Prior to that KHS indoor athletic events took place at what was called the municipal auditorium up Broadway.

KHS, which saw its population peak in the 1960s, has been at different times a three- and a four-year school. Myron J. Michael Junior High School, built adjacent to the high school in 1937 to relieve overcrowding, is now scheduled for demolition.

The school opened with the traditional three sports: boys' football, basketball and baseball, and girls' basketball. Girls' sports were given up after a few years, but resumed on a limited basis in the 1930s. The school now offers programs in some 20 sports for boys and girls.

Sports directors and coaches are the stuff of legend at KHS. Warren Kias (1946–1964) was the first man to hold the title of sports director. His teams won more than 50 championships.

The school song was composed by two students in 1917.

Among its thousands of graduates, which include doctors and nurses, lawyers and judges, business leaders, educators, administrators of every stripe and homemakers, KHS also claims three U.S. Army generals. Medal of Honor winner Robert Dietz was a member of the class of 1938. Arthur Flemming (Class of 1922), the first Federal Secretary of Health, Education and Welfare, served presidents from Franklin Roosevelt to Ronald Reagan.

An urban campus from its first days, academia is separated from busy Broadway by what is now a three-foot wall. Brett said the wall was some 15 feet high when it fronted O'Reilly's woods. The wall and Broadway's pavement were gradually reduced to their present levels over the years, according to City Historian Edwin Ford, KHS Class of 1936. For years, under the school's open-campus system, the wall was a hangout for students, for better or worse. "They liked to go down there and smoke cigarettes," Brett recalled. "In the sixties it might have been different smokes."

Edwin Ford

Some parents objected to their kids fraternizing around the wall. "One mother came to me and said she couldn't get her daughter to stop hanging out on the wall," Brett, who was then an assistant principal, said. "I suggested she go and sit on the wall with her daughter. She did, and that was the end of that."

Under the school's closed-campus system now in effect the wall is a desolate place. District security officers shoo off any students with a mind to hang.

The 100th anniversary celebration resumed the weekend of April 18–19, 2015 with a brunch at the high school cafeteria. There was "a walk through the decades," with each of the school's 11 decades represented by photos and artifacts in separate classrooms. There was a formal program in the auditorium with former principal William Dederick presiding. The KHS alumni choir performed. A cocktail reception was held at Hillside Manor Restaurant. On Sunday, April 19, the Creative Center for Education hosted a movement event at Dietz Stadium, featuring dances from the decades.

The original lecture was presented by educator Anna Brett on December 12, 2014.

30.

John Jay:
Model of Diplomacy

John Jay, American aristocrat, author of the state constitution, first Chief Justice of New York and of the United States, but perhaps more important, one of three ambassadors who negotiated the peace treaty with Britain in Paris after the American Revolution, was the subject of the thirtieth edition of "Kingston's Buried Treasures."

Ray Raymond, a career diplomat in the British Foreign Service, and now a professor of constitutional studies at SUNY Ulster, called Jay "America's founding diplomat," the title of his upcoming book.

John Jay (1745–1829) was a delegate to the New York State Constitutional Convention in Kingston during the spring of 1777 when its state government was drawn up and ratified. Ten years later Jay's work in Kingston played a prominent role in the creation of the United States Constitution, based largely on New York's, in Philadelphia. But it was Raymond's contention that Jay's greatest service to his country was as a negotiator at Paris with John Adams and Benjamin Franklin after the war.

John Jay

"America's founding diplomat"

As Raymond explained to his audience at the Senate House in Kingston, Jay understood that nations act in their own self-interest. It was therefore the duty of a diplomat to clearly understand and appreciate the positions of not only his own country, but of competing interests. That America signed a peace treaty with Britain, separate from its wartime French ally, was a result of that analysis.

Franklin, having represented American interests in France throughout the war, and largely responsible for recruiting France as an ally, was senior in the American peace delegation, but according to Raymond, was considered something of a Francophile after years of close association with the French. He was revered by France as one of the leading men of his generation. "Franklin needed no entrée, unlike Jay and Adams who had to establish themselves as diplomats," Raymond said. Adams and Jay served their apprenticeships in diplomacy as ambassadors to the Netherlands and Spain, respectively, during the latter years of the war.

Given the difficulties of communication, foreign diplomats in the eighteenth century "were pretty much on their own" once they arrived on station. Ambassadors were "powerful figures, custodians of vital information, trusted to act on it," Raymond explained.

Raymond said Jay understood that France and Spain, given their vast holdings on the North American continent, "wanted America to remain a small client state" in order to protect their interests. Jay saw America as a potentially strong, independent power. Britain sought to resume normal relations with America, what Raymond called a natural ally and a major trading partner before the war, while limiting French and Spanish influence in North America. Raymond termed the 1783 Treaty of Paris the most important treaty in American history.

Jay, Adams and Franklin came to Paris with a "very weak hand," Raymond told his audience, but with the clear purpose to play competing interests among European powers to the advantage of their fledging nation.

Jay was sent to London by Washington to negotiate what became known as the Jay Treaty in 1794, which many historians believe averted war with England for almost a decade. He returned to New York to serve as governor (1795–1801), where he signed legislation abolishing slavery in New York. Jay retired from public life to his 400-acre estate in Katonah in 1801. His wife, Sarah, a member of the Livingston family, died there shortly thereafter.

The original lecture was presented by SUNY Ulster Professor Ray Raymond on January 16, 2015.

31.

General Sherman V. Hasbrouck: Kingston and the Manhattan Project

Gen. Sherman V. Hasbrouck

General Sherman V. Hasbrouck, president of Kingston High School's first graduating class in 1916, was profiled at the thirty-first edition of the "Kingston's Buried Treasures" series at the Senate House Museum. Hasbrouck, whose army career spanned 37 years, was born in Stone Ridge in 1898 and died at 103.

Hasbrouck's life and times were presented by retired U.S. Army Lieutenant Colonel Sherman Fleek, who has served as West Point historian since 2009. Fleek, a graduate of Brigham Young University and a career army officer, was accompanied by two West Point cadets, David Koerper of Kentucky (2016) and Niquelle Cassador of Washington State (2017).

Hasbrouck's career at the military academy was typically rigorous, more so after America entered World War I in April 1917. At that point, Fleek said, an accelerated schedule was ordered at West Point due to a shortage of commissioned officers. Four classes were

A Commanding Presence

graduated in a year and a half, Hasbrouck's on November 1, 1918. The war ended 10 days later.

As Fleek explained it, half the class returned to academics after 60-day furloughs, and the other half entered active duty. Hasbrouck resumed his studies until May 1920. Among his classmates were legendary army football coach Earl "Red" Blaik and Lyman Lemnitzer, a future chairman of the Joint Chiefs of Staff. Fleek had no explanation for why Hasbrouck's photo and biography were not included in the Academy class of 1920 yearbook, which he passed around the audience. Hasbrouck was 142nd among 209 in his class.

There was no mention of Hasbrouck's intra-war service, but he was a decorated combat commander in an armored artillery division in Europe during World War II, where he fought in the Battle of the Bulge.

Hasbrouck's connection with the Manhattan Project (atomic bomb development) came during his service as Chief of Staff of the Armed Forces Special Weapons Project in New Mexico from 1946 to 1949. The army at the time was exploring tactical uses for atomic weapons.

He returned to New Mexico as deputy field commander of the Special Weapons Project for three years after service on the United Nations military staff. He retired as a brigadier (one-star) general in 1955.

Hasbrouck, a member the Hasbrouck family of New Paltz, had a lifelong interest in genealogy. He was a familiar sight around Stone Ridge during his long retirement and often participated in uniform in military events in Stone Ridge, Kingston and at West Point.

"He drove into town every day to pick up his mail well into his nineties," said longtime friend Vincent DeLuca of Kingston after Fleek's address. DeLuca and Hasbrouck shared a devotion to Army football and a love of the military.

"One time he skidded off an icy Buck Road in his truck and a state trooper pulled up to investigate," DeLuca recalled. "He [the trooper] asked the general for his driver's license. Noting his age, about 95 at the time, the officer asked if he should be still be driving." A commanding presence even at his advanced age, the irate general gave the young trooper a dressing-down. "The general told the trooper he still spanked relatives older than him [Hasbrouck had nine step-grandchildren] and that he should go back to his barracks. The trooper complied."

Hasbrouck was the oldest living West Point graduate when he died in 2001.

The original lecture was presented by Lieutenant Colonel Sherman Fleek on February 20, 2015.

32.

Arthur Wicks: The Cleaner Who Controlled the Senate

Sen. Arthur Wicks

Former state senator Arthur Wicks (1887–1985) is generally credited with forcing the location of the New York State Thruway on the west side of the Hudson River, but his road to political retirement led through Sing Sing Prison on the east side a decade later.

Wicks, "the cleaner who controlled the Senate," was the subject of the thirty-second edition of the "Kingston's Buried Treasures" series at the Senate House Museum.

As told to Kingston journalist Hugh Reynolds, Wicks, then chairman of the Senate Finance Committee, held up legislation in the Senate in late 1942 on the proposed Thruway until Governor Herbert Lehman agreed to reroute the superhighway from the east to the west side of the Hudson River. Wicks, in a 1971 interview with Reynolds for the *Daily Freeman*'s anniversary edition, said the economic impact has been

> *From a Corner Office in Kingston He Pulled the Strings of New York Government*

substantial. Wicks also warred with Governor Thomas Dewey over the construction of the Kingston-Rhinecliff Bridge, which Dewey initially vetoed.

Wicks was born in New York City and went as far as the sixth grade before his family moved to Olive in 1900 due to his father's tuberculosis. The family moved back to New York after the elder Wicks died.

Wicks married Mabel Everette of Olive in June 1909. He took correspondence courses in engineering, which got him work on the construction of New York City subways systems.

Wicks was a Democrat in Olive when he moved to Kingston in 1916, where he purchased the Thompson laundry. He became a Republican in 1922 after a falling-out with Democrats and ran for the first of 15 terms in the Senate from the Ulster-Delaware-Sullivan district in 1926.

He was appointed chairman of the Senate Finance Committee in 1941 and elected Republican majority leader in 1949. He held the position of Ulster County Republican Chairman from 1944 to 1957. Wicks filled a vacancy as acting lieutenant governor in 1953.

His clash with Dewey, for whom the Thruway was officially named in 1964, occurred over Wicks's visits to convicted extortionist and labor leader Joseph Fay in 1953 at Sing Sing Prison. Fay was serving an 18-year sentence for extortion at the time. Wicks said he was seeking Fay's assistance in resolving labor issues on the construction of the Thruway in his senate district.

Wicks (left) with Gov. Thomas Dewey (center)

Dewey called a special session of the Senate and demanded Wicks's removal from office. Wicks resigned as majority leader and declared himself vindicated. He ran for one last term in 1954 and retired. He stepped down as county Republican Chairman in 1957.

Wicks was known for his charitable work in Kingston, chairing major fundraising drives for the YMCA and Benedictine Hospital, and for advocating education. He personally paid the college expenses of 16 Ulster County youth. A scholarship in his name was established at Ulster County Community College. The A.H. Wicks volunteer fire company in midtown Kingston is named for him.

The original lecture was presented by journalist Hugh Reynolds on March 20, 2015.

33.

Old Stone Houses:
Our History in Stone

Spanning four centuries, Kingston's eclectic Stockade District is an example of architectural vernacular, building what is needed with the materials, expertise and labor at hand and the needs of the community.

So said Mark Yallum, a self-educated authority on Kingston's stone houses,

Persen House

speaking on the subject "Written in Stone: Ulster County's Historic Legacy" at the thirty-third edition of the "Kingston's Buried Treasures" series at the Senate House Museum.

Taking his overflow audience on a virtual tour of familiar historic stone houses in the Stockade District, many of them long gone, Yallum filled in the cracks on how these structures were built, burned and rebuilt and in many cases destroyed by the

> *"These buildings are a physical expression of our history."*

march of commercial progress over a period dating from the mid-seventeenth century to the 1960s. The images of some long-gone buildings are only preserved in photographs or period line drawings.

"These buildings are a physical expression of our history," said series moderator Paul O'Neill before introducing Yallum to what appeared to be a record audience of more than 100 people. "We have lost lots of them, but we have saved many."

Yallum said his interest in stone houses came at an early age. "We grew up in a stone house," he said. "We shared rooms with people who came before us, people long gone. The house was like a family member."

Kingston's first homes were made of wood, constructed along the Esopus Creek where early settlers tilled their fields with Native Americans. "To dispel a rumor, there were no log cabins in Kingston," Yallum said. The large stones plows uncovered were used to build the more substantial stone houses that occupied the Stockade area after it was constructed as a defensive measure around 1660. The first stone houses were typically one or two rooms with sleeping quarters on an upper level. Cooking was done in basement areas. Houses would be expanded as families grew. Clapboard houses were also built during the early period with slate (bluestone) and brick appearing as those industries rose in the area. As with the Old Dutch Church, Kingston was the mother of stone houses. Construction spread from Kingston generally southwest following fertile creekfront farmland. Yallum said there were about 240 stone houses in Kingston at the turn of the nineteenth century.

Three distinct eras (or events) impacted stone houses in Kingston, beginning with the British burning of the village in October 1777. Only the Van Steenburgh House on Wall Street at the head of Franklin survived out of some 300 building destroyed. The interiors and roofs of razed stone houses were rebuilt.

The Federal period between 1790 and 1820 produced considerable renovation of existing stone houses. Kingston's emergence as a mercantile hub after the Civil War had a direct impact on its

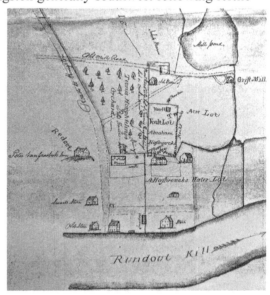

Early map of the Strand

buildings. Most of the stone houses on Wall, North Front and Fair streets were torn down for taller commercial buildings. "The Stockade was considered very high-value real estate," Yallum noted.

But it was early twentieth-century "progress" that cost the town most of its stone houses. It was cheaper and quicker to demolish a stone structure to build something larger and taller. The 200-room Stuyvesant Hotel on the corner of Fair Street and John (opened in 1911) is an example. "It was the Progressive era," Yallum said. "People believed that everything new was going to be better. The Titanic had not yet hit the iceberg."

On the residential side, installing modern electricity, heating and plumbing in a stone house was expensive. Sometimes the answer was a wooden addition, more often, demolition. "Some buildings just fell victim to fashion," Yallum said.

While the city had strict building codes in the early 1900s, before mid-century there was little law on the books in terms of historic preservation. There were scattered, sometimes individual efforts to preserve the city's architecture.

Around 1910, the Wiltwyck chapter of the Daughters of the American Revolution intervened when the new owner of the Lucas Elmendorf Mansion at 111 Green Street wanted to tear down what is now the eighteenth-century DAR House across the street (at Green and Crown) to establish an urban park.

DAR House

In the late 1930s, Kingston antiques dealer Fred Johnston convinced the Standard Oil Company not to purchase and demolish an eighteenth-century Federal clapboard home at Wall and Main to make way for a gas station. Johnston purchased the property and established his business there. An outspoken preservationist during his long career, Johnston willed the building to the Friends of Historic Kingston. The Johnston Museum is now its headquarters.

Fred Johnston House

Urban renewal demolition of the east side of Broadway between St. Mary's Church and the Rondout Creek in the mid-1960s galvanized the historic preservation movement. The construction of the modern six-story glass county office building at Fair and Main, once the site of a 1683 stone house, may have also been a factor. Critics called it "the glass menagerie." Friends of Historic Kingston was formed; the Kingston Landmarks

Urban Removal

Preservation Commission was legislated to strictly control renovation of historic buildings. One of their early triumphs was preventing uptown urban renewal from demolishing three historic buildings at the corner of Lucas Avenue and Green Street (one a stone house built by the county's first sheriff after independence in the 1770s) in order to improve traffic flow to the Wall Street commercial area.

Yallum suggested that strolling the Stockade area can be revealing. "Many stone houses have been disguised over time," he said. "They're still there, hiding in plain sight. We just don't know where they are."

Kingston, which calls itself the Colonial City, retains one of the largest collections of stone houses in the state, a key tourist attraction. Friends of Historic Kingston conducts regular Stockade walking tours.

Kingston City Historian Edwin Ford was in attendance; he celebrated his ninety-seventh birthday on April 15.

Abraham Masten House, demolished in the 1960's

The original lecture was presented by architectural historian Mark Yallum on April 17, 2015.

34.

Bootlegging:
Our Prohibition Past

During the Prohibition era, the Hudson Valley became an integral part of the "Bootleg Trail" from Canada to New York City and beyond. On May 15 author and historian Eleanor "Ellie" Charwat regaled a standing-room-only audience at Kingston's Senate House historic site on the Hudson Valley's tumultuous Prohibition past. It was the thirty-fourth installment of the "Kingston's Buried Treasures" lecture series.

Jack "Legs" Diamond

In 1919, the Eighteenth Amendment to the U.S. Constitution outlawed the manufacture and sale of intoxicating beverages in the United States. Cheered by the "drys" and bewailed by the "wets," Prohibition ultimately contributed to an erosion of public respect for the law and gave rise to a new form of organized crime. As the

A Thirsty History

nation moved into the Depression, the public's unabated thirst for illegal alcohol—and the Hudson Valley's prime location on the distribution line from Canada to New York City—created an environment readymade for participation in the illicit bootlegging trade.

According to Charwat, the Hudson Valley's agricultural economy made it an ideal location for the manufacture of bootleg booze. Made from almost any type of grain or fruit, illegal alcohol could be distilled by struggling farmers as well as by large-scale breweries in the predominantly rural setting. With large areas available for storage and ingenious methods of distribution, Kingston and the Hudson Valley soon came to the attention of famed mobsters such as Legs Diamond and Dutch Schultz. Located at the boundary line between the territories of the two racketeers, Kingston became at times the flashpoint for gang wars for control of the region's lucrative alcohol trade. (More recently, the Dutchess County farm where Schultz had his hooch made is now being used to distill legal sugar wash "moonshine.")

The Barmann Brewery off Fair Street Extension in Kingston was infamous during the Prohibition period. Under the control of Legs Diamond, the brewery was able to distribute its product to the various speakeasies and distribution centers through an elaborate system of hoses running throughout the Kingston sewer system; according to some sources, the services were provided by Kingston's fire department. When it was ultimately raided by authorities, the enormous amounts of illegal alcohol and cash confiscated led to its moniker as "The Million-Dollar Seizure."

Opposition to Prohibition, however, grew so strong that its repeal became a critical issue in the 1932 presidential election. Democratic candidate Franklin D. Roosevelt ultimately made the repeal of the Eighteenth Amendment a bedrock of his campaign and, in keeping with his word, its repeal was one of the first tasks of his administration upon election. The passage of the Twenty-first Amendment in 1933 finally ended Prohibition.

The original lecture was presented by historian Eleanor Charwat on May 15, 2015.

35.

The DeWitt Mill and the Sign of the Crocodile: A Forgotten Treasure

They never played "Crocodile Rock" at the early nineteenth-century Crocodile Inn on DeWitt's Mill road at the corner of Route 32 in the town of Hurley (at the time), but they probably danced the quadrille in its large kitchen or argued life-and-death colonial politics in the parlor.

The original building, a stone house constructed in 1736 by the father of Revolutionary War leader and patriot Colonel Charles DeWitt, was operated as the Crocodile Inn by his son Garrett (there are various spellings of his first name)

Dewitt House – The Crocodile Inn

An Unlikely Find Commands Big Money at Auction

for about 30 years until the mid-1830s. The mill across the road to the south was built by Colonel DeWitt and lasted into the 1850s. Like DeWitt, the house and mill played important roles in the Revolutionary War.

The Crocodile Inn was the subject of historian Gail Whistance's lecture at the thirty-fifth edition of the "Kingston's Buried Treasures" series.

The inn, a community meeting place, as were the DeWitt home and mill prior to and during the War of Independence, was distinguished by a large sign with a crude, handpainted crocodile.

By old Dutch custom, the crocodile featured at apothecary shops was apparently a symbol of clandestine drinking. There was also a natural stone outcropping in the basement of the inn that some saw as resembling a crocodile's tail, Whistance said.

"It's classic American folk art," Whistance told her audience at the Senate House Museum. "I doubt if the untutored artist ever saw a crocodile in his life." But the sign was (and is) a rarity, she said, perhaps one of "very few" among the more than (estimated) 50,000 tavern signs that were handmade and painted on wood in the eighteenth and early nineteenth centuries.

That the crocodile sign survived at all was something of a miracle, she said.

After handing down the property through generations, the DeWitt family sold the original building around 1929, but kept the tavern sign. Two publications in the early twentieth century noted the sign in the house. The building was destroyed by fire in 1930.

The sign next reappears in 2004 when local auctioneer Jay Werbalowsky spotted it hanging on the wall at a home where he was auctioning its contents. The home's new owner had retrieved it from a pile of debris to be thrown out. Werbalowsky saw value in the piece and offered the owner "several thousand dollars," Whistance recounted. Refused, he offered to auction it.

Enter Jack Whistance, a noted Kingston antiquarian and history buff and Whistance's father-in-law.

"A bold bidder," according to his daughter-in-law, Whistance outbid rivals from several museums and dealers for what *Arts and Antiques* magazine called "one of America's top 100 treasures" in 2008. Leslie Keno, of Keno twins of *Antiques Road Show* fame, called it "an iconic piece."

Whistance paid $247,000 for the sign, including buyer's fees.

Jack Whistance died in mid-2007 and his son Bruce (Gail's husband) commissioned Sothebys to sell the sign. It did not meet the reserve price. Whistance later sold it to a private collector "somewhere in the Northeast," Gail Whistance said. She declined to divulge the selling price.

"It's a wonderful thing the sign was saved, given its connection to one of Ulster County's most prominent families," said lecture moderator Paul O'Neill. "Hopefully, it may come back to Ulster County someday where it belongs."

Whistance echoed those sentiments. "Although Jack did not get his wish to keep the sign in Ulster County," she said, "he would have been very pleased to know how many people have heard about the sign and the history behind it."

Gail Whistance apologized to the audience for some of the gaps in her story, explaining, "When you search history you don't always get all the answers you want." She was praised by O'Neill for "reconnecting one of our most important families to modern times."

Whistance, who presented this lecture to the Hurley Historical Society in 2011, also spoke to the history of the DeWitt family, in particular Colonel Charles DeWitt, a member of the Continental Congress, soldier, statesman, and framer of the New York State Constitution.

DeWitt's mill was located across the road from the family home. It was unique in that the spring-fed stream that ran the mill never froze in winter. It was the only mill in the county that operated all year long. General George Washington called on Governor George Clinton to supply flour to his starving army at Valley Forge in the severe winter of 1777–1778. Flour from the DeWitt mill and pork were hauled by oxen to Valley Forge. "Sadly, the oxen did not return," Whistance said. Washington commended local farmers (including DeWitt) for their service during a brief visit to Hurley in November 1782.

Mill stone at DeWitt House

The original lecture was presented by Gail Whistance on June 19, 2015.

36.

The Cordts of Kingston:
Providing the Building Blocks of a Nation

The old expression "built like a brick [outhouse]" spoke to the durability and the desirability of Hudson Valley bricks during a century when products produced on the shores of the river were the building blocks of cities, especially New York, along the eastern seaboard. One of the leading Kingston brickmakers of the day was the Cordts family, whose history was detailed by former Alderman Hayes Clement at the thirty-sixth edition of the "Kingston's Buried Treasures" series.

John H. Cordts (center) and workers

John H. Cordts, born in 1823 in Hanover, Germany, emigrated to this country at 14. A dozen years later he partnered in a brickyard in Cornwall, Orange County, which led in 1865 to his partnership with William Hutton of Kingston to create the Cordts and Hutton brickyard in East Kingston. Remnants of the brickyard, which ceased production in the 1980s, can be seen off Kingston Point.

The Hudson River Valley, which Clement called "the Silicon Valley of its day," was

> **"The Silicon Valley of its day"**

ideal for brickmaking, combining loam and clay with pulverized anthracite coal delivered from Pennsylvania by the D&H Canal. Ready transportation to its major market in New York City was available via the river and by rail.

After five years in business the Cordts and Hutton brickyard was producing more than 10 million bricks a year—it reached 18 million at the turn of the century—but not just any old building (interior) bricks. The company was noted for its facing bricks, which sold at a premium price. The Cordts and Hutton legacy can still be viewed from the sidewalks of New York and other cities.

At peak production, the brickyard employed some 115 men, almost three times more than its nearest local competitor. Skilled workers were paid two or three dollars a day, unskilled, $1.25. Most brickyards operated for six months a year, laying off their workers during cold weather. Cordts and Hutton, with superior technology, ran for eight months and gave interest-free loans to retain skilled workers. "There was a high degree of worker loyalty," Clement noted.

Cordts and Hutton business interests were a complex web. Cordts ran the brickyard while Hutton focused on his lumber and hardware business in Ponckhockie. Cordts was a founder of two banks and also invested widely in local real estate. The partners divided their holdings in 1887, with Hutton taking over the brickyard and Cordts keeping the real estate and banking. Cordts died at home in 1891 after turning the business over to his son, John N. Cordts (1865–1913).

The other Cordts legacy is the magnificent home John H. Cordts built in 1874 atop Lindsley Avenue in the northeast corner of the city. The 8,300 square foot, 30-room Edgewood Terrace looms high over Ponckhockie on 15 landscaped acres—Cordts's version of "living above the store," according to Clement. Its views of the Hudson and Rondout Creek encompass the brickyard, East Kingston and Ponckhockie, where most of the company's workers lived.

The Cordts family took a keen interest in the civic, political and religious life of Kingston. The elder Cordts was a city alderman for 18 years, ending in 1890. His son, John N., a three-term state senator, was first elected on the Roosevelt ticket in 1904. According to Clement, Cordts ran some 900 votes ahead of the president in Ulster County. Teddy Roosevelt handily defeated Democratic candidate Alton Parker of Esopus.

The elder Cordts, as one of the leading residents of the village of Rondout, would undoubtedly have had a strong voice in the merger of Kingston and Rondout to form the city of Kingston in 1872. City Hall on Broadway was built at the same time as Cordts's mansion. John N. managed the family's extensive real estate holdings—they owned most of Fair Street from John to Main—and was a cofounder of the Stock and Cordts furniture company.

The family was of mixed faith, with the founding Cordts a German Lutheran and his wife a Catholic. Cordts, "though not particularly religious," according to Clement, was a founder and a benefactor of the Evangelical Lutheran Church on Livingston Street; his wife was a supporter of St. Joseph's Roman Catholic Church on Main Street. Their daughter Katherine taught at the parochial school for many years.

Clement, a local realtor who ran unsuccessfully for mayor in 2011, demonstrated extensive knowledge of a town he settled in only about ten years ago. He showed a deft sense of humor about urban legends to an audience of about 100 regulars at the Senate House Museum on Fair Street.

As an example, he told the gathering that in December 1900, John N. Cordts was among the state electors who officially certified President William McKinley's second term. McKinley was killed by an assassin in Buffalo in September 1901. Legend has it that McKinley stopped by the Cordts mansion "for his last meal" before departing for Buffalo the next day, Clement said, to nods from the history-steeped audience.

"But that's not true," Clement said after a pause, to loud guffaws. "McKinley went directly from Washington to his home in Ohio and then to Buffalo." Another legend of the Cordts mansion is that the room where McKinley "ate his last meal" (apparently he didn't breakfast in Buffalo) was preserved as it was for generations. "Not true, either," Clement said.

After a fire in 1986, the mansion passed from the hands of Cordts descendents. Left vacant for many years, it ran through several owners before being acquired by prominent New York City artist Hunt Slonem about ten years ago. Slonem has since restored the mansion to its Second Empire magnificence, complete with period furnishings and decoration.

The Cordts were a congenial lot, according to Clement. Many residents knew members of the family, in particular Florence Cordts, one of John N.'s children who lived into the mid-1980s. Katherine Cordts, a beloved teacher at St. Joseph's School, lived past 100. Living descendents include sisters Tildy Davenport of Stone Ridge and Carol Heine of Kingston. Heine attended the Clement lecture, where she regaled attendees with stories about family gatherings in her youth at the mansion in Ponckhockie. Her family lived on West Chestnut Street. She praised those in attendance for their interest in maintaining Kingston's legacies. "You are just as important as we were," she said, to sustained applause.

The Cordts and Huttons are buried in Montrepose Cemetery with other nineteenth- and twentieth-century Kingston moguls.

The original lecture was presented by former Kingston Alderman Hayes Clement on July 17, 2015.

37.

Robert Dietz:
Kingston and the Medal of Honor

I t was a story often told of a citizen soldier from Kingston who battled across France, Belgium and Germany as a squad leader with his armored division, ultimately losing his life and winning the Medal of Honor in an attack on an enemy fortified position five weeks before the end of World War II in Europe.

But Daniel Joyce, who recounted the life and heroism of Kingston's only Medal of Honor winner, Army Staff Sergeant Robert Herman Dietz, at Kingston's thirty-seventh edition of its "Buried Treasures" series last week, also spoke to Dietz's difficult boyhood in midtown Kingston, his kindness to many and what those living 70 years after his death can do to honor his heroism.

Robert Dietz

Joyce, a native of Kingston who now lives in Cairo, Greene County, is a retired postal worker, who for some years was assigned to the Broadway Post Office where Dietz and thousands of Kingstonians joined the armed forces. Dietz, a 1940 graduate of Kingston High School enlisted in the army in March 1942. He was awarded the Bronze Star

> *"Ordinary people sometimes do extraordinary things."*

and the Purple Heart medals before the action on March 29, 1945 at Kirchhain, Germany that led to the Medal of Honor. He is buried in Wiltwyck Cemetery.

"Sergeant Dietz is an example that heroes do exist among us, that ordinary people sometimes do extraordinary things," program moderator Paul O'Neill told an audience of about 100 at the Senate House Museum on Fair Street.

Dietz was born in 1921. His father, Herman Dietz, was severely gassed in World War I and suffered respiratory ailments for most of his life. After his mother died when he was 12, Robert Dietz lived on Abbey Street with his father. Dietz helped care for his younger sister, Dorothy, who had moved to live with an aunt on South Manor Avenue. Dietz worked at his father's gas station and hamburger stand on Broadway prior to the war.

From the testimony of contemporaries Dietz was described as a quiet, unassuming youngster. His Kingston High School yearbook spoke to his "determination" to carry out tasks. One of Dietz's boyhood friends was Homer Terwilliger from nearby Clifton Avenue, who had crippled legs. Dietz often carried Terwilliger to high school on his back and later rigged a car so Terwilliger could drive it. Dietz was described as strong and athletic. Due to family circumstances, he did not participate in after-school sports, but he was known to run daily from his home in midtown Kingston to where the Adams store is now located in the Town of Ulster.

Dietz shipped to Europe in June 1944 and was assigned to the 7th Armored Division—the "lucky 7th"—which landed in France in August 1944. The 7th was engaged in heavy fighting—Dietz was wounded in September—and was one of the units assigned to the Ardennes section of Belgium, France and Luxembourg to rest and refit when the Germans launched a major offensive on December 16, 1944, the Battle of the Bulge. The 7th is credited with holding up the German advance, which allowed Allied forces to bring in reserves and drive the Germans back.

The action in which Dietz was awarded the Medal of Honor took place on the bridges leading to the small German town of Kirchhain, 40 miles east of the Rhine River. The Germans had mined and fortified the bridges with machine guns and *panzerfausts* (bazookas). Dietz, according to his Medal of Honor citation, single-handedly attacked the bridges, killing numerous defenders and wading into the water to detach mines. He was killed by an enemy volley as he stood to wave his squad forward.

"In a sense, Sergeant Dietz carried his squad on his shoulders that day," Joyce said in reference to Homer Terwilliger.

Major General Robert Hasbrouck (KHS 1917), Dietz's division commander, credited Dietz with shortening the war by at least a week and thereby "saving thousands of lives."

"I was one of those lives that Bob Dietz saved," said Bill Ford of Kingston, who was in combat in Germany with another division at the time of Dietz's action. Ford is the younger brother of Kingston City Historian Ed Ford, also a World War II army veteran.

Strategically, the 7th's taking of Kirchhain cleared the way for the division to capture the nearby 230-foot Eldersee dam, thwarting German efforts to blow the dam and flood the Ruhr Valley. Doing so would have held up the Allied advance in that area. Shortly after Dietz's action, an entire Panzer corps surrendered to the 7th, according to Hasbrouck.

Dietz was buried in Germany. His remains were returned to Kingston in October 1948 and re-interred with full military honors next to his mother in Wiltwyck Cemetery. His father, Herman Dietz, was murdered in 1966 in a holdup at his store on Hasbrouck Avenue and is also buried in the Wiltwyck Cemetery plot.

In conclusion, Joyce said Dietz should be honored and remembered by citizens exercising their civic duties. "If you have no other reason to vote, go out and vote in memory of Sergeant Dietz and all those who served and sacrificed for us," he said. He said schoolchildren should be taught about Dietz's heroism and that the city should formally recognize Dietz every March 29.

The original lecture was presented by Daniel Joyce on August 21, 2015.

38.

The DAR House:
Kingston's Crossroads of History

Kingston's seventeenth-century DAR House stands on a slight promontory at the triangular intersection of Crown and Green streets, what some call "the crossroads of history." But after surviving the 1777 burning of Kingston by the British, the stately two-story stone colonial was almost demolished to make way for a community garden at the turn of the twentieth century. It was saved and restored by the Wiltwyck Chapter of Daughters of the American Revolution and now serves as the Chapter's meeting house.

Wiltwyck Chapter of Daughters of the American Revolution current meeting house

These and other tales of what was for more than a century called "the Tappen House" and a history of its occupants were presented by DAR member Nancy Chando at the thirty-eighth edition of the "Kingston's Buried Treasures" lecture series.

Chando, a retired school teacher and an active member of the DAR, traces her ancestry to the Tappen family through her mother, the late Terry

> *After Surviving the Burning of Kingston, the Historic House Was Almost Demolished to Make Way for a Garden*

Beckert, née Houghtaling. Chando wove a history of the DAR House, its owners and their various activities before a crowd of well over 100 at the house itself. It was only the second time the Senate House-sponsored lecture series has not been held in the Senate House Museum, though Senate House staff provided folding chairs for the DAR event. A lecture by City Historian Edwin Ford was delivered offsite at Montrepose Cemetery.

Like most of Kingston's remaining colonial stone houses, the DAR House, built by Antoine Crispell perhaps as early as 1670, began as a small, one-story structure with a kitchen and two or three rooms. Later additions, including a second story, are undocumented but evidenced by the stonework in its exterior walls. The interior was extensively renovated in the early twentieth century.

The unusual junction of Crown and Green streets is shown on a 1695 English map, the house facing the apex of the Crown-Green triangle. The rear of the house may have contained a barn or a stable, typical of the time. In later years that part of the property featured lavish gardens, mentioned in several historical accounts.

Crispell occupied the house until 1705, when he sold it to Mathys Van Keuren, the husband of his granddaughter. Its closely held ownership was repeated through the centuries with Jansens, Sleights and (mostly) Tappens detailed on deeds secured from county archives and displayed by Chando. "All the grantors were related to all the grantees," she said.

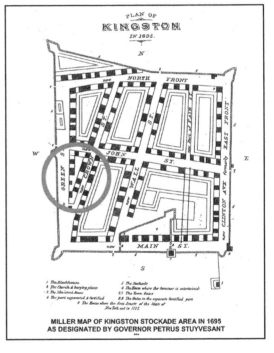

MILLER MAP OF KINGSTON STOCKADE AREA IN 1695
AS DESIGNATED BY GOVERNOR PETRUS STUYVESANT

Members of the Tappen family held the property for 102 years, ending in 1907 when John Kenyon, son of Christina Tappen, granddaughter of John R. Tappen, sold the house to the DAR. John R. Tappen, a lawyer and son of Christopher Tappen, George Clinton's deputy and successor as county clerk, published the weekly Ulster County *Plebeian* during the mid-nineteenth century in the building, with offices and printing presses on the second floor. The building also served as a book and stationery store at one time and was the site of weekly farmers' markets. Burned by the British in 1777, but with relatively light damage, the house was quickly restored.

Because house owner Hendricus (Henry) Sleight was president of the Kingston village board of trustees at the time, Chando surmised that George Washington was probably hosted there during his visit to Kingston in 1782. "It would have been likely for Washington to call on one of the more prominent village residents," she said.

None of its latter-day owners lived in the house. At times it was a boarding house. The house was vacant during periods of the 1890s, leading to its decline.

A wealthy Mrs. Marguerite Walker Westinghouse, wife of George Westinghouse Jr., inventor of the railway air brake, was living in the Lucas Elmendorf House across Green Street at the time. She apparently considered the vacant Tappen House "an eyesore" and declared her intention to secure the property, demolish the house and plant public gardens for her viewing pleasure.

The Wiltwyck Chapter of DAR, founded in 1889, stepped up. In 1907, the Chapter purchased the property for $2,300 ($54,000 in today's dollars) and retained prominent architect Myron Teller for restoration and renovation. One of the features of Teller's interior renovation was a replica staircase taken from Washington's Mount Vernon home. Teller also created large meeting rooms and added front and rear porches and a shed over an entrance to the cellar. Teller later supervised the restoration of Kingston City Hall after a 1927 fire gutted the building.

The 90-member Wiltwyck DAR maintains the house through endowments, investments and fundraising and with what Chando called "careful financial management." The house, a veritable museum of Kingston history, is open to the public for special occasions several times a year.

The original lecture was presented by historian Nancy Chando on September 18, 2015.

39.

General Robert W. Hasbrouck: Hero of the Battle of the Bulge

Gen. Robert W, Hasbrouck

Hasbrouck and Jansen avenues in Kingston are named for the Hasbrouck families, but it was the leadership of General Robert Hasbrouck Sr. and his 7th Armored Division at the Battle of the Bulge in December 1945 that made him a war hero. Hasbrouck's son, Robert Jr., recounted his father's career from his birth in Kingston in 1896 to his almost 30 years' military service at the thirty-ninth edition of the "Kingston's Buried Treasures" series at the Senate House Museum.

Robert Hasbrouck Jr., 81, like his father was a graduate of the U.S. Military Academy at West Point and rose to the rank of captain during his six years in the army.

An Unsung Hero in Hitler's Final Push to Win the War

He was a Vice President with Chase Manhattan and is currently president of the Hasbrouck Family Foundation.

The Hasbrouck family dates to the early eighteenth century in Kingston; its forebears were shipping merchants and bankers in Rondout. Hasbrouck

Park and Jansen Avenue are named after Jansen Hasbrouck, Robert Sr.'s grandfather. The future army general was born on Walnut Street in Ponckhockie and was a member of the last class of Kingston Academy in 1914. He was a cousin to army General Sherman Hasbrouck of Stone Ridge, a member of the first graduating class of Kingston High School.

Hasbrouck Sr. was Medal of Honor recipient Sergeant Robert Dietz's commanding officer and signed the recommendation for the medal after Dietz was killed in action on March 29, 1945. Hasbrouck, who retired from the army for health reasons in 1947, spoke at dedication ceremonies when Dietz's body was returned from Germany to Kingston for reburial in 1948.

The scholastic careers of the two Hasbrouck cousins were cut short by the exigencies of World War I and its urgent need for army officers. Both graduated about a year ahead of time in August 1917 and saw service in France. For Robert Hasbrouck, wartime promotion came quickly. He jumped two ranks to captain before the war ended, but waited 19 years for a promotion to major between the wars. During that period Hasbrouck graduated from the Army War College and married a "Southern belle," Marjorie Nightingale, at West Point. He was promoted to lieutenant colonel in 1940 and assigned to select army mobilization sites as the war in Europe escalated. He was a colonel in two army armored divisions before General Omar Bradley ordered him to take command of the 7th Armored Division in Holland. He was a member of General Bradley's staff that planned the invasion of Normandy.

Following heavy fighting in Holland, Hasbrouck's unit was sent to Aachen near the Dutch-German border to refit as the winter of 1944 approached.

"Little did they or anyone else on the Allied side know that a fierce battle for survival was about to begin in a so-called 'quiet sector' of the Ardennes," Hasbrouck told his audience.

Four German armies, two armored, broke through lightly defended American positions in the Ardennes at dawn on December 16, with a goal of reaching Antwerp, Belgium, within a week and dividing British and American armies. Legend surrounds the "Battlin' Bastards of Bastogne" in the southern shoulder of the bulge, but it was at St. Vith where the German advance was delayed and eventually reversed.

General Courtney Hodge's First Army was ordered to the defense of St. Vith, about 50 miles south of Aachen, which both sides considered the strategic point of the battle, on the northern shoulder of what would become known as the Battle of the Bulge. St. Vith was a communications center of numerous crossroads and the only rail line between Germany and Belgium.

Hasbrouck's 7th Armored Division and three other divisions held out for five days.

The Battle of the Bulge

"Little did they or anyone else on the Allied side know that a fierce battle for survival was about to begin in a so-called 'quiet sector' of the Ardennes."

Historians have concluded the strategic delay caused by the defenders of St. Vith wrecked the Germans' tight timetable and effectively decided the outcome of the battle. German commander General Hasso von Manteuffel advised Adolph Hitler to abandon the attack after his forces stalled at St. Vith. Hitler refused, continuing a battle which officially ended in late January 1945. Americans suffered some 80,000 casualties, the worst of the war. By comparison, Allied casualties were estimated at 10,000 during the Normandy invasion.

Robert Hasbrouck was awarded the Silver Star, Bronze Star and Distinguished Service Medal for his wartime service.

The badly mauled 7th Armored was refitted and led the breakout into Germany from Remagen Bridge in March 1945. The unit's website stated it captured more than 100,000 Germans before the war ended in early May. The 7th reached the Baltic Sea on May 3,

Gen. Hasbrouck receiving his Distinguished Service Medal

leading to its unit slogan, "from the beaches [of Normandy in August 1944] to the Baltic." The unit took an estimated 5,800 casualties, including 1,400 killed in action or missing during its 272 days in combat.

Reassigned to the United States in August 1945 after the war as Chief of Staff of Army Ground Forces, Major General Hasbrouck was afforded a unique honor by his men of the 7th Armored, according to his son. "His troops (about 10,000 men) stood at attention on both sides of the highway to the airport as he departed for home, offering him a final salute of respect and admiration," Hasbrouck said of his father. "I'd like to think the old (49 at the time) general had tears in his eyes." Hasbrouck attended almost every reunion of the 7th Armored Division Association after the war. He was inducted into the Armor Hall of Fame in 1976.

Hasbrouck retired from the army in 1947, but a year later served on the postwar Hoover Commission, which recommended among other things a restructuring of the armed forces and the establishing of the office of Chairman of the Joint Chiefs of Staff. Omar Bradley, Hasbrouck's former commanding officer, was the first to hold that position. Hasbrouck was a co-founder of the Federal Service Finance Corporation, which catered to service members' financial needs. He worked with military historians on the war in Europe and according to his son was always available to assist his former soldiers on issues involving government services, documents, etc.

Hasbrouck died in 1985 and is buried at West Point.

Robert Hasbrouck Jr., who traveled from Summit, New Jersey, for his lecture, displayed some army humor to an audience of about 100, revealing that many people felt his granite-jawed father bore a strong resemblance to actor Randolph Scott. "The family certainly thought so," he said.

The younger Hasbrouck said he doubted if his father knew Staff Sergeant Dietz, one of thousands of men under his command.

Hasbrouck Jr. said he was assigned as an army officer in the late 1950s to the section of the Ardennes and to the same unit where Germans burst through in 1944. "I was hoping the same thing did not occur again" (with the Soviets), he said with a smile.

"We've now had two Hasbroucks and a Dietz," moderator Paul O'Neill said in thanking Hasbrouck for his remarks.

The original lecture was presented by Robert Hasbrouck Jr. on October 16, 2015.

40.

The New York State Constitutional Convention: The Foundation for a Nation

Gouverneur Morris, John Jay and Robert Livingston

Three men in a room" has become a pejorative term for how power is exercised in state government, but it was three remarkable young men in a front room in the Ulster County Courthouse in Kingston who wrote, in secret, New York's first constitution in 1777.

Called the "foundation of a nation" for its influence on the Federal Constitution adopted in Philadelphia 10 years later, the story of the state's founding document was told by retired Court of Appeals Judge Albert M. Rosenblatt of Poughkeepsie at the fortieth edition of the "Kingston's Buried Treasures" series at the Senate House Museum. The museum, erected in 1927, was built of the same fieldstone as the courthouse (built between 1732 and 1737) and is located only a few blocks from where patriots met to finalize the first constitution.

A Band on the Run Forms a State and a Nation

John Jay, 31, became first Chief Justice of the United States and is generally considered the main author of the state constitution. He was the oldest of the three-man committee appointed to draft the document by a 13-man committee. Chancellor Robert Livingston and Gouverneur Morris were 27 and 24, respectively. While relatively young men, Rosenblatt described them as well-educated lawyers steeped in English law and political philosophy.

Rosenblatt, 79, is a former Dutchess County district attorney, county judge, Supreme Court judge and member of the state's highest court, the Court of Appeals.

The Constitutional Convention, which comprised about 100 delegates from the colonial Provisional Congress, was much a band on the run. "Chased up the Hudson Valley by the British," according to Rosenblatt, delegates settled in Kingston on March 7, 1777.

They began deliberations in the village's most prominent building, the courthouse on Wall Street, under what Rosenblatt described as grueling conditions. The courthouse basement was also the county jail, where Tories were kept in primitive confinement. "They ran the criminals out and put in the Tories," Rosenblatt told his audience. The stench, the former judge said, wrinkling his nose, was unbearable, leading delegates to smoke heavily—the original smoke-filled room? Given the difficulties of travel in colonial times and the threat of marauding British, loyalists and Indians, and wartime duties, there were seldom more than 40 delegates in attendance at any time.

The final document was approved 32–1, with Peter Livingston the lone dissenter, on Sunday, April 20, and read to the populace on the courthouse steps two days later. Jay, whose mother had died in Westchester County on April 17, did not attend. Ulster resident Charles DeWitt was a member of that committee. DeWitt and Jay were featured in previous "Kingston's Buried Treasures" lectures.

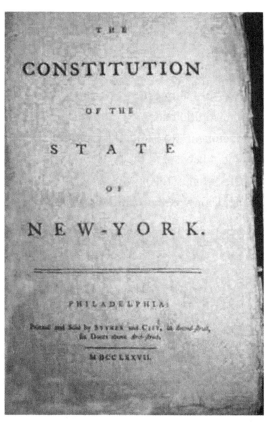

The state constitution, like the federal, called for three branches of government and a separation of powers, but unlike the Constitution adopted in Philadelphia, gave basic rights of freedom of religion and assembly, the right to bear arms and equal protection under the law to New York citizens. Those rights, advanced by New Yorkers and other states, were included in the first amendments to the U.S. Constitution, the Bill of Rights. New York's federal ratification convention was held at Poughkeepsie in 1788 where delegates, led by Governor George Clinton, held out for a bill of rights.

With the minimum of nine states having already ratified—New York, New Hampshire and Virginia were among the last—"New York faced some difficult choices," Rosenblatt told his audience. "They could either ratify the Constitution, join Canada or go it alone as a separate country." With some assurances from federalists that a bill of rights would be immediately added to the new Constitution— it was among the first acts of the new government—New York relented but only by two votes.

Program moderator Paul O'Neill, in "thanking our distinguished guest speaker," summed up the founding of the state in New York with, "They did it. We're glad they did it. And we're glad they did it here."

Like the Federal Constitution, the New York version was very much about limiting the powers of the executive, which at that time was equated with kingly authority. The "republican" form of government they created for the first time vested power in the people and it was in the assembly, "the house of the people," where that power was exercised. As an example, the original constitution created a "Council of Appointment" comprised of four senators elected annually by the assembly, which had veto power over the governor's appointments. The Council was abolished by constitutional amendment in 1822, the first constitution to be directly voted on by the people.

The original constitution was noteworthy also in that it described Native Americans as "persons" to be treated fairly. There were minor revisions to the constitution by statute in 1801 under Governor John Jay, but the original remained substantially in effect until a convention in 1821. There have been nine constitutional conventions, the last in 1967. The constitution itself allows the legislature to recommend conventions, approved by the people, every 20 years. Voters rejected a convention in 1987; it was not offered in 2007. New Yorkers do not have the right of direct referendum.

The original courthouse, probably of wood, was built around 1683, the stone courthouse begun in 1732 and burned by

Kingston Courthouse in which the 1777 Constitution was promulgated

the British in October 1777. The familiar modern stone structure was restored between 1816 and 1818. Additions were added in 1834, 1868, 1897 and 1899 (the jail). Its interior was extensively renovated in the 1980s after a new jail was constructed on Golden Hill in Kingston.

O'Neill, the county's Commissioner of Jurors, also announced, to the surprise of many in an audience of more than 100, that the next lecture in January would be the last of the monthly series, begun over three years ago. "All good things must come to an end," he said in thanking the dozens of people who had a part in the series, its lecturers and its faithful audience.

The original lecture was presented by retired Court of Appeals Judge Albert Rosenblatt on November 13, 2015.

41

Lost Rondout:
A Story of Urban Removal

The final version of the documentary *Lost Rondout: A Story of Urban Removal* was shown to an enthusiastic audience at the Senate House Museum, coincidentally the last installment of the long-running "Kingston's Buried Treasures" series.

"It was entirely appropriate that we should end our series with this outstanding work," said "Buried Treasures" founder and moderator Paul O'Neill. "It tells us we need to preserve our history before it's too late," he said in praising filmmakers Stephen Blauweiss and Lynn Woods for their work. The film was shown free of charge to a record audience of about 150 people.

The first installment of the monthly "Kingston's Buried Treasures" series in September 2012 featured a lecture on the life of Kingston founder Thomas Chambers and continued on a monthly basis to include 39 speakers on subjects ranging from notable Kingstonians to where some of them are buried, the rise and fall of local industries, local journalism, prominent buildings and visiting notables including George

> *"On one side were these beautiful buildings and on the other, nothing. I wondered what happened to them."*

Washington, George Clinton and John Jay, reflecting the city's status as the first state capital.

The lectures were filmed by Bob Rizzo of Port Ewen and will still be available on DVD "a hundred years from now," predicted O'Neill.

Senate House site manager Tom Kernan presented O'Neill with a replica from the museum's extensive Civil War collection of a pass given to General George Sharpe by Robert E. Lee in April 1865 after the Confederate surrender at Appomattox. Sharpe, a native of Kingston, was the subject of one of the "Buried Treasures" series.

Rondout and Kingston were separate villages before merging to form the city of Kingston in 1872. In some ways, they suffered similar disasters. Kingston was burned by the British in 1777, but quickly recovered. The 16-acre section east of Broadway in Rondout was demolished via urban renewal in the late 1960s and remains largely vacant. Kingston lost 6,000 residents between the 1960 and 1970 censuses.

For more than a century a teeming, noisy, polluted waterfront (pigs once ran in the streets), "Broadway East," as it was designated under the federal urban renewal plan, was reduced to empty grassland in less than four years. Some 450 buildings, which ranged from three-story brick tenements to single family homes and over 90 businesses, were taken down, beginning with the demolition of a two-story nineteenth-century home on Hanratty Street in February 1966. Despite commitments to renewal, the only thing built there was a City Hall in the early 1970s, relocated from central Broadway to attract development and to settle the city's $1 million debt with the federal government. A row of condominiums was built on lower Broadway in the late 1980s, followed by some restaurants and the establishment of the Hudson River Maritime Museum in one of the few buildings left standing.

Blauweiss said he was stunned by the contrast between nineteenth-century architecture (though obviously rundown) on the west side of Broadway and the empty fields across the street when he first came to Kingston some 30 years ago.

"On one side were these beautiful buildings and on the other, nothing," he said. "I wondered what happened to them." He moved to Kingston from New York with his family a few years later.

Woods, who has lived on Hone Street a few blocks from the urban renewal area for some 20 years, met Blauweiss about five years ago but had had similar thoughts. Under the original urban renewal plans that included blocks west of Broadway, her house would have been taken.

The catalyst for what became the *Lost Rondout* film was Kingston native Eugene Dauner, who as a young man prowled the still-standing Rondout area with his camera in all seasons, recording for posterity most of the still-standing buildings, many with the dreaded circle with a line through it designating imminent demolition. The producers also made extensive use of period photographs by Jack Mathews and former *Freeman* photographer Bob Haines. The film is dedicated to Dauner, who was in attendance for the screening.

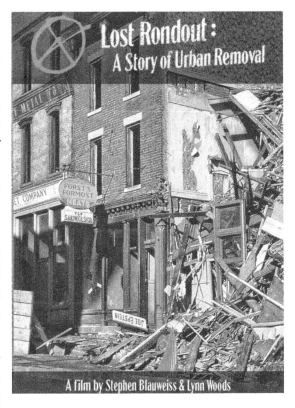

Woods said she started thinking about a book on Broadway East around 2009, did some research, but put it aside for a while. The seeds of the Woods-Blauweiss collaboration—he the award-winning film maker with a bent for urban architecture, she the investigative reporter forever digging for material and subjects—were planted in 2013 at the Anvil Gallery on North Front Street. The two had known each other casually for several years but, given their respective interests, had never worked on a joint project. Woods, who had thought about a book on the lost Rondout, urged Blauweiss to take in a showing of Gene Dauner's photographs the following week. "I was blown away," he said.

More conversation led to a conclusion that their respective talents, along with music by Peter Wetzler (who joined in 2014) and Dauner's photos, could produce something special. That something special was Woods rounding up local people who had lived in Rondout and had experienced firsthand those events. Government leaders also commented on policy decisions that produced what some called an "urban disaster."

Their first uncut "work in progress" screening of the film was shown in the fall of 2014, "to great enthusiasm and excitement," recalled Woods.

Joe Van Dyke, son of "old Rondout's last alderman," was one of those featured in the film. His father, Leonard Van Dyke, fought urban renewal on behalf of his constituents, most of whom were living then in the Broadway East area.

Showing the film as a work in progress produced more material and greater perspective,

Wood said. But not without some risk, said Blauweiss. "We were very vulnerable," Blauweiss said. "People who knew the history raised a lot of questions about what we included, what we left out, facts and such. I think it took a lot of guts on our part to do it that way, but it made for a much-improved product."

Woods said she felt reactions were for the most part positive. "It was more a process of delving deeper and creating more context with each new version," she said.

As word spread, others came forward with stories and material, filling in gaps, opening different areas for exploration. "The best thing about the last showing was that nobody asked any questions," Blauweiss said.

After advancing some of their own money to get the project started, the producers raised more than $20,000 with their limited showings. Their showing of the film at the Rosendale Theater drew a full house and turned away numerous attendees.

In its final version, *Lost Rondout* is less parochial, more the story of any American small town that had undergone extensive urban renewal in the 1960s, more about social upheaval and racial relations, changing views on urban planning, more marketable on a broader scale.

As one observer said after the Senate House showing, "Mistakes were made, obviously, a neighborhood was destroyed. That was 50 years ago, in a different time. You can't apply our values to that time."

Woods and Blauweiss plan to present their 70-minute film to a few film festivals and to pursue television and educational options. Woods said state officials have expressed interest in the film's historical value.

The original lecture and film were presented by filmmakers Lynn Woods and Stephen Blauweiss on January 15, 2016.

Kingston's BURIED TREASURES

42.

IBM: Then and Now

By Hugh Reynolds

As the focus of this series was on historical figures and events, IBM's 40-year period, ending in 1994, was not part of the original series. However, upon reflection it was agreed that IBM's impact on the community warranted its inclusion in this publication. We thank Friends of Historic Kingston for sponsoring its IBM series and for making this material available for this book.

"Kingston The IBM Years"

IBM then and now. Like many of a certain age in the region, I come from an IBM family. My mother and her siblings were IBMers, as were two uncles by marriage. They were of the generation that first worked at "the plants" in Kingston and Poughkeepsie. I worked briefly at IBM Poughkeepsie as a contract employee before entering the field of journalism.

We thank Friends of Historic Kingston for sponsoring its IBM series

IBM represented what in time might be considered the last "industrial age" for the greater Kingston area. First there was agriculture, then coal, bluestone and cement, then for a while garment factories, then IBM.

We want to thank the Friends of Historic Kingston for permission to reprint this excerpt from the book where it originally appeared, *Kingston The IBM Years.* Black Dome Press. 2014.

As in many things, IBM's coming to Kingston was a combination of opportunity, luck and timing, or so said a former city water superintendent.

I dropped by the water department on a slow news day to find Superintendent Ed Cloonan in a nostalgic mood. IBM, at the time—around 1970—was in one of its expansion modes. There were some concerns about adequate water supply for the new buildings they were planning, thus my visit.

Cloonan told an interesting story.

About a year before IBM's advance men (in those days) came to town, Cloonan was paid a visit by another team from another major manufacturer. They were interested in building a new plant. They'd needed at least 200 acres, which Kingston didn't have, and at least a million gallons of potable water a day, which Kingston had in abundance.

The Kingston water system, connecting Cooper Lake in the Town of Woodstock to the city via the Town of Ulster, had been established in the 1890s. Expanding to meet a growing city's needs, it had not been professionally surveyed in years. Cloonan, seizing the opportunity, convinced the ultra-conservative water board to approve an engineering study of the entire system, one designed to accurately gauge capacity and delivery systems. It took about a year and produced a state of the art, up to date document.

The impetus for the survey went elsewhere, but a year later, an IBM advance team paid a call on the superintendent. They were looking to locate a plant and they needed proof of adequate water supply.

Cloonan told me he went to his filing cabinet and pulled out the voluminous engineering report. The team flipped through the report, expressed their admiration for the department's attention to detail, and impressed asked if they could borrow it overnight. "You guys are really on the ball," Cloonan said they told him.

The terms were reasonable to both parties. Kingston would supply the company's Town of Ulster complex with up to 1 million gallons of water a day (which they rarely used) at agreed-to premium prices. All necessary connections to the existing water system would be paid for and maintained by IBM.

The ensuing construction boom was not confined to the 500 acres the plant occupied in Lake Katrine.

Witness the major public construction that took place circa 1954–94.

The Thruway was completed in the mid-50s with exits at Kingston, New Paltz and Saugerties. Route 84, the Kingston-Rhinecliff Bridge and the Newburgh-Beacon Bridge were all completed within 15 years of IBM's arrival.

The Kingston school system was consolidated in 1959, followed by the construction within five years of all its schools, except for the high school. Schools were built in Onteora, Saugerties, Rosendale, Esopus and Red Hook.

Ulster Community College was created; SUNY New Paltz was expanded.

The county office building and a new city hall were constructed.

Both Kingston hospitals underwent major expansions, with IBM as a generous contributor.

Kingston Plaza was followed by massive regional shopping malls in the Town of Ulster.

Kingston-Ulster airport expanded.

Middle income housing sprang up in Whittier, Rolling Meadows, Barclay Heights, Tillson and Red Hook.

Some of this would have taken place without IBM, but all of it?

IBM's was a paternal culture. It is interesting to note that on IBM job applications, one of the last questions asked was if the applicant had a relative working for IBM.

The company took care of its people and that loyalty was reciprocated. IBMers had their own country club, traveled together on company-sponsored trips, participated in company social events, athletic leagues. The company cafeteria offered good food at good prices. The company had its own security and firefighting forces.

While the company hired most of its workforce locally, it also infused the population with outside talent. It offered opportunity to advance within its system. It recognized and encouraged community involvement by its employees. It employed local tradesmen and artisans whenever possible. And it rarely quibbled about the price of things.

IBMers, homegrown products for the most part, were of the community, deeply involved in most of its affairs, but separate. The "loaned executive" program helped many a non-profit, United Way for the most part, reorganize, recruit volunteers and reach goals.

Plant security was the byword, the rule, and for good reason. IBM Kingston began by making computers for the government, principally the defense department. It was called FSD for Federal Systems Division.

I once asked a friend of mine who had a "good job" at IBM, exactly what he did. He had some kind of title like production engineer expeditor. "To tell you the truth," he said, "I'm not exactly sure and when I begin to figure it out, they transfer me to another department."

Employees wore badges with their photos, names and department emblazoned thereon.

Visitors were rarely out of the sight of their company escorts.

There were jokes about IBM standing for "I've Been Moved," but in most cases a transfer was a requirement for promotion. There too the company took care of its people.

Market value on homes of those transferred was guaranteed, a significant boost to the local real estate industry.

IBM liked to project itself as a "good neighbor." It was located on Neighborhood Road, after all. It paid its taxes without protest, creating something of a tax haven in the Town of Ulster. The company did not get involved with local controversies, though its employees were encouraged toward civic activity, including holding public office. Two mayors of Kingston were IBMers.

IBM left Kingston in 1994, but as with most things with IBM, the planning for the move started many years earlier.

Here's a story.

In late 1985, WTZA opened its studio in Kingston at 721 Broadway. It was a gala event, much like a Hollywood premiere, with all the town's leading lights in attendance. Governor Mario Cuomo was guest of honor.

The Great Orator, speaking in his extemporaneous style, offered a few platitudes on why a new television station linking the Hudson Valley from the Tappen Zee Bridge to Albany (thus TZA) was important to the economic and cultural growth of the region.

He concluded by speaking of a meeting he had had recently at IBM headquarters in Armonk with company CEO Jack Akers. Akers, some may recall, was the IBM executive who did not have a computer in his office.

"From the CEO's office in Armonk, you can see Connecticut, perhaps 500 yards away," Cuomo said (and I'm writing from memory here). "I asked him if his company had any plans to move across the border." Akers's response, the governor said, was "IBM has no plans to move out of Kingston."

The collective gasp at this "good news" was as if something had sucked all the air out of the room. That IBM had even *thought* about moving from Kingston was unthinkable, unimaginable.

It being close to my 11 p.m. deadline, I rushed back to the paper to file my story. The headline read "IBM says it has no plans to leave Kingston." One can only imagine the reactions around kitchen tables and diners the next morning, not to mention at IBM.

An IBM public relations man called me shortly after I arrived for work around 8:30 the next day.

"What kind of journalism do you practice over there?" he demanded. "You write a story about IBM and you don't call IBM for comment?"

"For one thing," I told him, "you guys are all gone by 5 p.m. I was writing at 10:30.

More importantly, when the governor of the state makes a statement in front of 250 people, we take it to the bank."

Mollified, but hardly satisfied, he offered me his private number to call "any time, day or night, anytime you write anything about IBM." He did not reiterate that IBM had no plans to move out of Kingston.

IBM employment peaked in Kingston at about 8,000 workers in 1988. At the time, the county had a workforce of about 60,000. These were among the best, most secure jobs. I think it's fair to calculate that at $40,000 per job, plus another $10,000 in benefits, IBM was generating some $400 million in annual payroll at its peak. Economic development specialists tell us the multiplier effect of manufacturing is on the order of almost two to one, meaning the financial impact approached a billion dollars a year.

But IBM's impact over a 40-year period on this region was much more than that. The company offered good wages in an area notorious for sweat shops. It was only about two generations removed from the advent of IBM when local workers were paid less than a dollar a day, while owners and managers resided in million-dollar mansions (adjusted for inflation) on hills overlooking the waterways. Was it no wonder then the company's location to this area was so strenuously opposed by local Brahmins?

A few days after IBM formally announced it was closing its Kingston plant—after years of pointed denial—Lt. Governor Stan Lundine came to town. "It will take time," he said to a group of glum-looking local officials.

IBM has been gone for almost 25 years now. Foiled in the hope that a so-called "state of the art" manufacturing plant would soon attract another major employer, the community has pursued a policy of diversity.

There is nostalgia about the IBM days when jobs were plentiful, businesses thrived, opportunities abounded, and restaurants were full, an appreciation made all the more poignant by what the community has become without its main benefactor.

Hugh Reynolds has been a working journalist in Ulster County for more than 40 years, first with the daily newspaper and later as a publisher of a weekly newspaper. He is currently a columnist/reporter employed by Kingston-based Ulster Publishing, which publishes the weekly newspapers in Woodstock, New Paltz, Saugerties and Kingston.